D1613455

THE GOLFER'S MISCELLANY

Interesting Facts, Feats,
and Extraordinary
Occurrences in the Royal
and Ancient Game

HARPER & ROW, PUBLISHERS

NEW YORK, EVANSTON, SAN FRANCISCO, LONDON

THE GOLFER'S MISCELLANY

EDITED BY
Percy Huggins

FOREWORD BY
George Plimpton

DRAWINGS BY
Bob Bugg

Text reproduced from *The Golfer's Handbook,* published annually at 94 Hope Street, Glasgow, Scotland.

THE GOLFER'S MISCELLANY.
Copyright © 1970 by Munro Barr Publications Limited
Illustrations Copyright © 1971 by Robert Bugg
Foreword Copyright © 1971 by Harper & Row, Publishers, Inc.

FIRST U.S. EDITION

STANDARD BOOK NUMBER: 06-011979-9

LIBRARY OF CONGRESS CATALOG CARD NUMBER: 73-138735

Designed by Lydia Link

Contents

Foreword

The Golfer's Handbook has been an institution in British golfing circles almost since it first appeared—which was over sixty years ago. The regular edition is a very thick volume indeed, over a thousand pages, a vast number of which have been excised by the editors for this present "export" volume. Gone are the advertisements; a directory of British and Continental golf clubs (which includes the names of greens keepers) with addresses of near-by garages, etc.; the endless lists of tournaments (there is one called the Carnoustie Craws Nest Tassie) and tournament winners (Miss M. Muttukumarasvami was the runner up in the Ceylon Ladies' Championship in 1963); trade directories; the conditions for various trophies such as the British Boys Amateur championship; a list of driving ranges in Ireland; and so forth. Purists who wallow in trivia may bemoan the loss of these pages. I myself miss the Rules of Golf which constitute the first pages of the regular edition; my appreciation of them is based largely on the nicety of having the rules lead off with a section on etiquette even before the fundamental definitions, and that they can be read for both education (after all, one should know the rules and most don't) and enlightenment (did you know that a worm is defined as a "loose impediment"?).

But no matter. What *is* included in these pages is the particular delight of *The Golfer's Handbook*—a lengthy section entitled "Interesting Facts, Feats, and Extraordinary Occurrences in the Game." The contents itself is enough to whet the reader's appetite: Freak Matches; Birds and Animals Interfering with Golf Balls and Attacking Players; Dark, Playing In; Balls Hit to and from Great Heights, etc. My own favorite category is Hit by Ball —Distance of Rebound, in which measurements of wayward ricochets (usually off caddies' foreheads) are solemnly recorded. The world's record is 75 yards, established on September 28, 1913, at the 7th hole of the Premier Mine Golf Course in South Africa. The caddy (who survived and indeed continued the round) is not listed by name, but the brand name of the ball is. It was a "Colonel."

The pleasure of browsing through almanacs, record books, catalogues, guides, and so forth, rises in direct proportion to the mental pictures that the text can provoke. *The Golfer's Miscellany* abounds in catalytic passages of great variety—all of them inducing fine bursts of pleasant contemplation. Indeed, the danger of getting into the *Miscellany* is that the reader finds that it is extremely difficult to extricate himself—rather like being imbedded in a very deep pot-hole bunker. Ah, but the pleasures of that bunker! I envy the reader who is looking into this collection for the first time.

GEORGE PLIMPTON

THE GOLFER'S
MISCELLANY

How Eighteen Holes Became a Round

The full complement of nine or eighteen holes is not traditional. Bruntsfield Links in the heart of the city of Edinburgh, the oldest course in the world where golf is still played, used to have only six holes, North Berwick seven, Gullane thirteen and later fifteen, Musselburgh five and later eight, the usual match being over two rounds or sixteen holes, and Montrose twenty-five. At Wimbledon, from 1864 to 1870, the full course was seven holes; when Tom Dunn went to the course he enlarged it to nineteen holes. Blackheath had seven holes, and the usual match there was three rounds to make twenty-one holes. Royal Aberdeen, as late as 1875, only had fifteen holes.

When the first open championship was played at Prestwick in 1860, the course consisted of twelve holes, and three rounds were played to complete the thirty-six holes, which was the championship test until 1891.

At St. Andrews the game for generations was played nine holes out, and the same nine greens were used for playing home. The accidental incident that eighteen was the most convenient number of holes at St. Andrews, with the gradually established preeminence of the place in golf, operated in the direction of eighteen holes being accepted as the standard number for a round of golf.

The smallest golf course is the three-hole links on the Isle of May in the Firth of Forth.

1

Balls Hit to and from Great Heights

In 1798 Edinburgh golfers undertook to drive a ball over the spire of St. Giles's Cathedral, Edinburgh, for a wager. Mr. Sceales of Leith, and Mr. Smellie, a printer, were each allowed six shots and succeeded in sending the balls well over the weathercock, a height of more than 160 feet from the ground.

Some years later Mr. Donald M'Lean, an Edinburgh lawyer, won a substantial bet by driving a ball over the Melville Monument in St. Andrew Square, Edinburgh, height 154 feet.

The three feats recorded above were done with feather balls.

Tom Morris in 1860, at the famous bridge of Ballochmyle, stood in the quarry beneath and, from a stick elevated horizontally, attempted to send golf balls over the bridge. He could raise them only to the pathway, 400 feet high, which was in itself a great feat with the gutta ball.

Captain Ernest Carter, on 28 September 1922, drove a ball from the roadway at the first tee on Harlech Links against the wall of Harlech Castle. The embattlements are 200 feet above the level of the roadway, and the point where the ball struck the embattlements was 180 yards from the point where the ball was teed. Captain Carter was laid odds of £100 to £1.

Oxford University golfers in 1928 hit golf balls from Brasenose quadrangle over the Bodleian Library. The danger to precious windows in the ancient buildings was recognized, and the feat was not again attempted.

In 1896 Freddie Tait, then a subaltern in the Black Watch, drove a ball from the Rookery, the highest building of Edinburgh Castle, in a match against a brother officer, to hole out in the fountain in Princess Street Gardens 350 feet below, a distance of about 300 yards.

Long drives have been made from mountain peaks, across the gorge at Victoria Falls, from the Pyramids, high buildings in New York, and on many occasions a golf ball has been driven into a passing train, and after traveling long distances been duly restored; but these are essentially freakish, and have been repeated so often that even the strangest need not be accorded a place in the authentic records of the game. As an illustration of such freakish "drives," a member of the New York Rangers hockey team, from the top of Mount Edith Cavell, 11,033 feet high, drove a ball which struck the Ghost Glacier 5,000 feet below and bounced off the rocky ledge another 1,000 feet. A total drop of 2,000 yards.

Disqualification and Withdrawing after Winning

In the Schweppes Championship, 1968, Brian Bamford exceeded the five-minute search for his ball and played it when found. He was disqualified. His round of 68 would have led the field.

Maurice Bembridge was disqualified in the first round of the

PGA Close Championship, 1968, owing to his caddie's action. The latter "found" the ball in the rough and Bembridge played it, but some way farther on his own ball was discovered. The caddie admitted that he had deliberately dropped a ball in the rough, and Bembridge sacked him on the spot and reported the matter to the officials.

In the 1966 U.S. Pensacola Open, Doug Sanders had a 4-stroke lead at the halfway stage after rounds of 63 and 67, and while being interviewed in the Press Room was summoned to the PGA quarters to be informed that he had not signed his card. It was shortly afterward intimated that he had been disqualified in view of the fact that players had been reminded before the event that, under the rules, they would not be searched for to sign their cards. The penalty was automatic disqualification.

Archie Compston was disqualified in the U.S. Open Championship, 1932, for being late, and in the 1941 championship Johnny Bulla was disqualified for starting before his time.

J. J. McDermott, the U.S. Open Champion, 1911–12, arrived for the British Open Championship at Prestwick in 1914 to discover that he had made a mistake of a week in the date the championship began. The American could not play as the qualifying rounds were completed on the day he arrived.

An amusing case was that of a competitor in the British Amateur Championship at Prestwick in 1922. He boarded the train at Ayr thinking it stopped at Prestwick, but it did not halt until Troom, some miles farther on. The railway runs alongside the first hole at Prestwick, and the player frantically yelled from the train that he would be back as soon as he could, but that was of no avail.

In the British Amateur Championship at Sandwich in 1937, Brigadier-General Critchley, arriving from New York on the *Queen Mary,* which had been delayed by fog at Southampton, flew by specially chartered airplane to Sandwich. He circled over the clubhouse, so that the officials knew he was nearly there; but he arrived six minutes late, and his name had been struck out. At the same championship a player, entered from Burma, who had traveled across the Pacific and the American continent and also was on the *Queen Mary,* traveled from Southampton by motor car and arrived four hours after his starting time to find, after journeying more than halfway round the world, that he was "struck out."

At the Irish Professional Championship at Hermitage, 1943, E. J. Hackett, Portmarnock professional, who tied for fourth place, reported to the committee that during the interval he had practiced on one of the greens. He was disqualified. At the Open Championship at St. Andrews, 1946, John Panton, Glenbervie, in the evening practiced putting on a green on the New Course, which was one of the qualifying courses. He himself reported his inadvertence to the Royal and Ancient Golf Club, and he was disqualified.

At the British Amateur Championship, Hoylake, 1953, play was officially suspended owing to a thunderstorm and rain which flooded the greens for one and one-half hours. Competitors were advised not to leave the clubhouse so as to be in readiness to start when play became possible. When the official order was given to restart, two competitors who had been present at their original times did not answer when called by the starter, and they were disqualified.

In the 1957 American Women's Open Championship, Mrs. Jackie Pung had the lowest score, 298 over four rounds, but lost the championship. The card she signed for the final round read "5" at the fourth hole instead of the correct "6." Her total of 72 was correct, but the error, under rigid rules, resulted in her disqualification. Miss Betty Jameson, who partnered Mrs. Pung and also returned a wrong score, was also disqualified.

One of the most sensational disqualifications ever was that of Roberto de Vicenzo in the 1968 U.S. Masters Tournament. Tom Aaron, with whom he was paired, mistakenly marked a 4 on Vicenzo's card for the seventeenth hole, and a total of 66, which should have been 65. In the excitement of the finish, Vicenzo unfortunately signed the card and so was deprived of a first-place tie with Bob Goalby and a play-off for the $20,000 prize.

Spectators Interfering with Balls

Deliberate interference by spectators with balls in play during important money matches was not unknown in the old days, when there was intense rivalry between the "schools" of Musselburgh, St. Andrews, and North Berwick; and disputes arose in stake matches caused by the action of spectators in kicking the ball into either a favorable or an unfavorable position.

Tom Morris, in his last match with Willie Park at Musselburgh, refused to go on because of interference by the spectators, and in the match on the same course about forty years later in 1895 between Willie Park, Jr., and J. H. Taylor, the barracking of the crowd and interference with play was so bad that when the Park-Vardon match came to be arranged in 1899, Vardon refused to accept Musselburgh as a site.

In more modern times the growth of the crowds at all important games leads to many instances where balls are inadvertently interfered with. In a memorable tie between Bobby Jones and Cyril Tolley in the 1930 British Amateur Championship at St. Andrews, Jones's approach to the seventeenth green struck spectators massed at the left end of the green and led to controversy as to whether it would have gone onto the famous road. In some views it would, in others it would not. Jones himself had deliberately played for that part of the green and had requested

stewards to get the crowd back. Had the ball gone onto the road the historic Jones Grand Slam of that year—the Open and Amateur Championships of Britain and the United States—might not have gone into the records.

In 1912 in the last round of the final of the British Amateur Championship at Westward Ho! between Abe Mitchell and John Ball, the drive of the former to the short fourteenth hit an open umbrella held by a lady protecting her from the heavy rain and, instead of landing on the green, the ball was diverted into a bunker. Mitchell, who was leading at the time by two holes, lost the hole, and Ball won the championship at the thirty-eighth hole.

In the match between the professionals of Great Britain and America at Southport in 1937 a dense crowd collected round the fifteenth green waiting for the Sarazen-Alliss match. The American's ball landed in the lap of a woman who picked it up and threw it so close to the hole that Sarazen got a 2 against Alliss's 3.

Highest, Lowest, and Coldest Golf Courses

Highest golf course in Europe is at Sestriere in the Italian Alps, 6,500 feet above sea level. It has eighteen holes and is reached by buses which climb from the railway station of Oulx by a winding road to the top of the pass. The highest golf courses in Great Britain are Llandrindod Wells (1,000–1,100 feet); Leadhills

(1,500 feet); Kington, Herefordshire (1,200 feet); Church Stretton, Shropshire (1,250 feet); and Tredegar (1,200–1,300 feet, on the mountain Cefn-y-Brithdir in Glamorgan).

The highest golf course in the world is the Tuctu Golf Club in Peru, which is 14,335 feet above sea level.

Golf 1,000 feet above the level of the summit of Mount Blanc is recorded by Captain F. E. S. Adair, who in his book *A Summer in High Asia* tells how, crossing the passes into Tibet, he camped one day at a lovely spot carpeted with short, bright green turf on the margin of a lake. This was the first time that the royal game had been played at an elevation above 16,000 feet.

Lowest golf course in the world is at Kallia, south of Jericho. It has nine holes, 1,250 feet below normal sea level. The course runs along the northeastern shores of the Dead Sea, and was made by the Kallia Hotel.

Although shut in for three years amid the eternal snow and ice of the Antarctic, Arbroath golfer Munro Sievwright did not neglect his practice with club and ball. His luggage included three clubs and a dozen red golf balls. In the light of the midnight sun he hit adventurous shots along the white wasteland on "fairways" of hard-packed snow. Munro, a physicist at the Antarctic Survey Base at Halley Bay, won the Carnoustie Craw's Nest Tassie in 1962, and was on the Edinburgh team which won the Scottish Universities Championship in 1963.

Balls Colliding and Touching

Playing in a four-ball match at Royal Guernsey Club, in June 1966, all four players were near the thirteenth green from the tee. Two of them—D. G. Hare and S. Machin—chipped up simultaneously; the balls collided in mid-air; Machin's ball hit the green, then the flagstick, and dropped into the hole for a birdie-2.

In May 1926, during the meeting of the Army Golfing Society at St. Andrews, Colonel Howard and Lieutenant-Colonel Buchanan Dunlop, while playing in the foursomes against J. Rodger and J. Mackie, hit full iron shots for their seconds to the sixteenth green. Each thought he had to play his ball first and, hidden by a bunker, the players struck their balls simultaneously. The balls, going toward the hole about 20 yards from the pin and 5 feet in the air, met with great force and dropped either side of the hole 5 yards apart.

In 1928 at Wentworth Falls, Australia, Dr. Alcorn and Mr. E. A. Avery of the Leura Club, were playing with professional E. Barnes. The tee shots of Mr. Avery and Barnes at the ninth hole finished on opposite sides of the fairway. Unknown to each other, both players hit their seconds (chip shots) at the same time. Dr. Alcorn, standing at the pin, suddenly saw two balls approaching the hole from different angles. They met in the air and then dropped into the hole.

On 10 August 1935, on the second hole at Southport and Ainsdale, F. M. Hargreave and T. Fletcher played their drives a distance of 270 yards, and the balls were touching.

In May 1950, W. S. Montford and David Murdoch, playing a club-championship tie at Greenock, found the balls from the tee touching in the middle of the fairway of the 363-yard twelfth hole. Then at the fifteenth hole (425 yards) the balls were again lying together from the tee shots. This time they were lying so close that a pencil could not be passed between them.

At Sunningdale, May 1930, in the London Inter-Club Four-some Tournament, at the short eighth the army and navy ball was driven into the bunker; J. E. Mellor, playing for the Royal Thames Yacht Club, sent his tee shot into the same bunker. To the amazement of the players, Mellor's ball was seen to pitch immediately on top of his opponent's in the bunker and rebound onto the green, so that he was able to get a 3 by this extraordinary "rub of the green."

In May 1953, four members of Southport and Ainsdale Golf Club, L. Birkett, E. G. O'Shea, F. Brewer, and H. Standish, in a four-baller, after playing their second shots at the third hole (378 yards), found three of the balls on the green touching each other just like a clover leaf.

Curious Scoring

Three threes, four fours, five fives, and six sixes is the only progressive combination that can work out for eighteen holes. A player in a South African competition had this sequence and noticed the curiosity in scoring.

Mr. R. H. Corbett, playing in the semifinal of the Tangye Cup at Mullim in 1916, did a score of 27. The remarkable part of Mr. Corbett's score is that it was made of nine successive 3's, par being 5, 3, 4, 4, 5, 3, 4, 4, 3.

On 2 September 1920, playing over Torphin, near Edinburgh, Mr. William Ingle did the first five holes in 1, 2, 3, 4, 5.

At Roehampton in the Limbless Ex-Servicemen's Association Open Mixed Foursomes, Miss Anne Sims and Mr. John Campbell, playing together, holed out from the tenth to the fourteenth respectively in 6, 5, 4, 3, 2. The fifteenth is 500 yards so there was no chance of completing the sequence with a 1.

Playing at Addington Palace, July 1934, Mr. Ronald Jones, a member of Hendon Club, holed five holes in 5, 4, 3, 2, 1. Jones had played a round in the morning, and in the late afternoon he engaged in a further nine holes with Max Rittenberg. The first four holes were in ordinary figures. The fifth was a par, the sixth in 4, one under par. On the seventh (391 yards) he holed a long putt for a 3, at the eighth (316 yards) he holed his approach for

2, and at the ninth (234 yards) the ball was short but ran forward to dribble into the hole for a 1 and give the player a "straight five but downward" to finish.

In July 1949 at Barassie, Irvine Rayenspark in the semifinal round of the Scottish Foursomes Tournament against Ranfurly Castle had every digit from 1 to 7. The 1 was at the seventh hole, 165 yards. The ball was wedged between the flagstick and the hole. This hole in one had the immortality denied to so many others for a press photographer was standing by the green and took a photograph. The 7 was at the fifth hole.

Two threesomes who joined forces at the Mohawk Country Club, Tulsa, Oklahoma, 1938, got the 147-yard fourth hole in 1, 2, 3, 4, 5, 6, the ace being recorded by Harold Nenninger, the club professional.

In a four-ball match in 1936, Mr. Richard Chapman partnered by Joe Ezar, the "clown" prince of golf, against the Honorable Michael Scott and Bobby Locke, then 18 years old, were four down and five to play. Ezar asked Mr. Scott if he had ever seen five birdies in a row. Mr. Scott replied that he could not recall that happening, and so Ezar made a bet on the same and pulled the match out one up by shooting five birdies—a truly remarkable achievement—to win the match.

A double eagle and an eagle at the same hole, neither player using his putter: playing the fifth hole at Goring and Streatley, Mr. F. T. Arnold holed his second shot (No. 2 iron). His partner, Mr. Noel Baker, holed his third (chip shot), but the eagle-3 was no match for the double eagle-2.

14

Extraordinary sequences of "one putts" occur with great frequency. A remarkable achievement in this connection was by F. Bebb, in a four-ball match at Bowring, Liverpool, May 1932. He had twenty-one putts on eighteen greens, fifteen single putts, and three of two each. The score was authenticated by R. Nelson, secretary, Liverpool and District Alliance, who played in the match.

Walter Hagen had the incredible achievement of seven putts for nine consecutive holes. He holed long putts on seven greens and chips at the other two greens.

What is believed to be a "world's record" of its kind was made at the Elks Country Club Golf Course, Elkhart, Indiana, on 31 August 1952. Mr. M. D. (Chick) Chatten, playing in a foursome with Messrs. Cawley, Meyers, and Sorg, had the almost unbelievable record of sixteen putts for an eighteen-hole round. This was accomplished by his taking only one putt on fourteen greens, two putts on one green, and holing three approaches. The putter he used was over twenty-eight years old.

At Four Lakes Country Club, Adamsville, Michigan, on 28 July 1966, Mrs. Paul (Betty) Thomas, Elkhart, Indiana, playing with Mrs. Peg Stone, in a Ladies' Day tournament (in which the number of putts is recorded), had twenty putts for her eighteen-hole round. She did this by taking only one putt on twelve greens, two putts on four greens, and holing two approaches.

Henry Cotton tells of one of the most extraordinary scoring feats ever. With some other professionals he was at Sestriere in the thirties for the Italian Open Championship and Joe Ezar, a colorful character in those days on both sides of the Atlantic, accepted a wager from a club official—1,000 lira for a 66 to break the course record; 2,000 for a 65, and 4,000 for a 64. "I'll do 64," said Ezar, and proceeded to jot down the hole-by-hole score figures he would do next day for the total. He accomplished the amazing feat exactly as nominated though he had actually to hole a pitch for his three at the ninth hole.

Miscellaneous Incidents and Strange Golfing Facts

A golfer in San Francisco played a stroke that landed his ball into a grassy overhang of a bunker. It was a lie needing special care, but while he leaned over for a close-up of the situation he sneezed, and his dentures falling out knocked his ball down into the bunker.

At Huddersfield a ball was cut in two by striking the edge of a scythe which a greenkeeper was holding in his hand.

Playing in a medal competition at Brodick, Isle of Arran, in October 1963, Mr. William Hartley, a clubmember, drove into a lagoon at the twelfth hole; took a No. 2 iron and got soaked while playing out his ball left-handed; then made his third shot with a No. 6 iron. The ball landed near the green, but the club slipped out of his wet hands and landed in the lagoon. Mr. Hartley arranged to drag the pool to recover his club.

16

In view of the increasing number of people crossing the road (known as Granny Clark's Wynd) which runs across the first and eighteenth fairways of the Old Course, St. Andrews, as a right of way, the Royal and Ancient Golf Club decided in 1969 to control the flow by erecting traffic lights, with an appropriate green for go, yellow for caution, and red for stop. The lights are controlled from the starter's box on the first tee. Golfers on the first tee must wait until the lights turn to green before driving off, and a notice has been erected at the Wynd warning pedestrians not to cross at yellow or red. This is regarded as a revolutionary step to control golfers.

Playing the second hole (105 yards) of the Daylesford (Australia) course, G. C. Hazen sliced his ball and struck a tree branch. The ball was deflected sharply onto the green, struck a magpie which was searching for worms, and, off the body of the stunned bird, rolled into the cup. An authentic magpie-eagle!

At the seventeenth green, St. Andrews, 4 May 1934, Lawson Little, in a practice game for the Great Britain-America match, had the extraordinary experience of a fine Persian cat trying to carry away his ball. A considerable number of spectators were following the match and observed the cat's antics.

At Geelong course, near Melbourne, Australia, while Mr. F. D. Walter was driving off, the strap of his wrist watch broke. The watch fell on the top of the ball at the exact moment of impact. The player picked up the watch unbroken 40 yards down the fairway.

In playing for the Hillhouse Cup, at Troon, in June 1907, Mr.

R. Andrew (who died in 1929) found his ball impaled on a hairpin. The hole cost him ten strokes. A similar occurrence happened at the opening of the new course at Bradford Moor a week or two later. Playing to the second hole H. A. Loveridge, the Shipley professional, on coming up to his ball found it impaled on a hairpin. Five putts were required to hole the ball, making seven strokes for the hole, the pin being too firmly embedded to be removed by a club during play. The Rules of Golf Committee subsequently decided that the hairpin could have been removed without penalty.

During the Royal and Ancient medal meeting, 25 September 1907, a member of the Royal and Ancient Club drove a ball which struck the sharp point of a hatpin in the hat of a lady who was crossing the course. The ball was so firmly impaled that it remained in position. The lady was not hurt.

F. G. Tait at St. Andrews drove a ball through a man's hat and had to pay the owner 5 shillings to purchase a new one. At the end of the round he was grumbling to old Tom Morris about the cost of this particular shot, when the sage of St. Andrews interrupted him: "Eh, Mr. Tait, you ought to be glad it was only a new hat you had to buy, and not an oak coffin."

Driving from the eleventh tee at the Belfairs Golf Course, Leigh, on 4 September 1935, the player heard a startled exclamation. Hurrying to investigate he discovered that his shot, at 160 yards distance, had smashed the pipe of a man taking a stroll over the course. The ball had cut the pipe out of the man's mouth without hurting him.

Bob Goalby, the U.S. Masters winner in 1968, won a tournament earlier that season while listening to a football match between shots on his transistor.

To miss the ball when playing a putt seems impossible, but there is more than one recorded instance. A mayor in an English Midlands town declared a course open, and he was asked to putt on the home green. Whether the crowd unnerved him or his "eye was out" is not known, but the mayor missed the ball completely. There never was a man who played better golf than Harry Vardon played in 1898 and 1899. All the same, at Wheaton, Illinois, in the U.S. Open Championship in 1900, which he won, he made the humiliating mistake of regarding a six-inch putt with such indifference that, in trying to knock it gaily into the hole, he missed the ball entirely, and struck his club into the ground, thus counting a stroke.

At the Scottish Professional Championship, 7 June 1939, at Culcabock, Inverness, J. M. Heggarty, professional of Cathkin Braes, was holing a putt of less than a foot when he struck the ball against his shoe, incurring a penalty of 2 strokes. The ball remained out of the hole, and Heggarty thus took 4 to hole out from about 10 inches.

A similar incident occurred at the eleventh hole at Troon in the 1962 British Open Championship. Max Faulkner carelessly tapped the ball against his foot, and the hole ultimately cost him eleven strokes.

At Rose Bay, New South Wales, 11 July 1931, D. J. Bayly MacArthur, on stepping into a bunker, began to sink. Mr. Mac-

Arthur, who weighed 14 stone, shouted for help. He was rescued when up to the armpits. He had stepped on a patch of quicksand aggravated by excess of moisture.

In the English Amateur Championship at Ganton in 1933, the winner, John Woollam, at one hole found his ball impaled on a thorn bush. Woollam played the shot with the ball rocking in the wind.

In his autobiography, Walter Hagen told of an extraordinary combination of coincidences. Playing in a championship practice round at Worcester (Massachusetts) he did the sixth hole in one. It was his first hole in one, it was the first shot played with a new ball, he used a No. 1 iron, and it was the first of July.

Abe Mitchell ended the final tie in the British Amateur Championship against John Ball in 1912 at Westward Ho! by catching the ball as it rose almost perpendicularly from the niblick shot he played out of a ditch at the thirty-eighth hole.

On 6 July 1938, Mr. N. Bathle, playing on Downfield, Dundee, was about to hit an iron shot when the ball was suddenly whisked away. Then the player was spun completely round. He had been caught in the fringe of a whirlwind. The whirlwind lifted a wooden shelter 60 feet into the air and burst it into smithereens over the eleventh green. A haystack was uprooted and a tree razed.

In a match over Queen's Park, Bournemouth, Archie Compston played a shot with his club at the full stretch of his arms, above his head. Finding that his ball had finished in the branches of a tree, Compston played a wonderful shot which almost reached the green.

Herbert M. Hepworth, Headingley, Leeds, Lord Mayor of Leeds in 1906, scored 1,000 holes in 2, a feat which took him 30 years to accomplish. It was celebrated by a dinner in 1931 at the Leeds Club. The first 2 was scored on 12 June 1901, at Cobble Hall Course, Leeds, and the 1,000th in 1931 at Alwoodley, Leeds. Mr. Hepworth died in November 1942.

At the Scottish Amateur Championship, Carnoustie, 1952, a player from the first tee hooked three drives into the burn and told his partner he was finished. The shortest "life" in a championship, a player giving up on the first tee.

The British Amateur Championship of 1895 was the last in which the final round was played over eighteen holes. The winner, Leslie Balfour (afterward L. M. Balfour-Melville) won his last three ties at the nineteenth hole, and each of his opponents, William Grey, Lawrence Auchterlonie, and John Ball (runner-up) put his respective approach shot into the Swilcan Burn and had to lift out and count a penalty stroke.

On the eve of the international match between Great Britain and the United States at Ganton, September 1949, objection was made by Ben Hogan, the captain of the American team, to the form and make of the iron clubs of two of the British players. There was a tense atmosphere for nearly five hours, while the clubs were examined and officials met. Eventually it was decided that, with some filing down, objections to the clubs would be withdrawn.

Overhead electric wires run along part of the second hole at Rondebosch, Cape Town. H. Hickson's tee shot struck one of the insulators 70 yards away and rebounded at a considerable height. Hickson ran back from the tee and caught the ball. In a cricket match this score might have read, "Hickson, caught and bowled Hickson . . . 0."

In the British Open Championship, 1921, at St. Andrews, Mr. Roger Wethered at the fourteenth hole in the third round, walking backward after studying the line of his putt, trod on his ball. He incurred a penalty stroke, which cost him the championship for he tied with Jock Hutchison at 296 and lost on the replay.

In the British Open Championship, 1889, at Musselburgh, Willie Park and Andrew Kirkaldy tied at 155. Park won on the play-off. In the second and final round of the championship—it was then decided over thirty-six holes—Kirkaldy's putt at the fourteenth hole stopped on the lip, not more than an inch from the hole. He made a one-handed stroke with his putter, missed the ball entirely, and this slip cost him the championship. Kirkaldy, great player though he was, never won the championship. He declared after missing the ridiculous putt, "If the hole was big enough, I'd bury myself in it!"

Playing on the Cumberland Golf Course, Sydney, November 1950, Mrs. D. Meakin sliced her tee shot into some trees lining the fairway, and the ball was eventually found in a fork in the branches of one of them. Mrs. Meakin deemed the ball unplayable and went back to play another. This shot was also sliced and, landing on the same place, the second ball knocked the first out of the fork of the tree onto the fairway. The incident was witnessed by three clubmembers.

A magnificent beech tree with a trunk 5 feet in diameter, which governed the approach to the fifth green at Killermont Golf Club, Glasgow, collapsed when hit by a ball driven by one of the clubmembers. It occurred during the 1939–45 war. There was hardly any wind to disturb the tree. When the ball hit the tree it was in full foliage and, for a moment or two, the tree trembled and then slowly collapsed. The story is told that it was the ball that knocked this tree down, but it may have been top-heavy. During the German blitzing of Clydebank, two land mines came down about 200 yards away, the tree was in the direct line of the blast of one of them, and the windows and doors of that side of the clubhouse were blown in. Bombing may have affected the tree, but certainly it was immediately following the blow by the ball that the tree fell down.

In the Scottish Amateur Championship at Carnoustie in 1967 Jim Hay, a Glasgow golfer, took up his stance at the fourteenth hole less than 2 feet away from what proved to be a live mortar bomb. Thinking it was only a smoke bomb, Hay decided that he could hit his shot without disturbing the object. Later an army official made the bomb, assumed to have been fired from the nearby military range in 1964, safe.

In July 1954 a golf shot came to the rescue of a man trapped on a small island by rising flood waters. Four men had been fishing from the island, but three had crossed to the mainland before the flood had reached its height. The fourth, Mr. Varley of Fleetwood, had waited a little too long and was cut off. Attempts to throw a rope had failed and Mr. R. Murray, the Wigtownshire Amateur Golf Champion who happened to be passing, produced a golf ball, drove a nail through it, and tied a piece of string to the nail. He then hit the ball, with a No. 8 iron, to the marooned man, who pulled the string, which was attached to a length of strong rope. This was hauled across the river and tied to a tree, and the angler crossed the river hand over hand.

Mr. Harry Leach, veteran member of St. Andrews Golf Club, had the longest "drive" of his golfing career on the Old Course, St. Andrews, on 26 May 1954. He drove from the first tee as a contractor's lorry was on the road which crosses the first and last fairways, and his ball landed in a load of debris which was being taken to the town dump at the end of the West Sands road. The driver was unaware of the ball joining the load and did not stop until he had reached the dump a mile away.

Competing in a tournament in South Africa, Dai Rees got red ants in his pants, and the big gallery was much amused at his antics in trying to get rid of them. The only way to do that apparently is to strip completely.

24

Hit by Ball—Distance of Rebound

Mr. R. J. Barton, Killiney Golf Club, County Dublin, playing at Machrie with Mr. W. C. Achfield, Chevin, Derbyshire, on 1 September 1913, was approaching the green of a blind hole 354 yards long, when his ball struck a caddie, named John M'Niven, on the head as he was replacing the flag in the hole. The ball rebounded 42 yards 2 feet 10 inches, which distance was measured twice in the presence of three people.

In the first round of the Los Angeles Open Championship, December 1952, a young amateur, Bud Hoelscher, with his second shot to the eighteenth hole hit a camera man on the head inflicting a scalp wound; the ball bounced to a can of water, from there it bounced against the face of the official announcer and fell on the green about 40 feet from the hole.

At Blairgowrie links, August 1908, a player on the tenth tee was hit on the head by a ball played to the ninth hole. The ball rebounded a distance of 34 yards, the distance being measured.

Playing over the Premier Mine Course, South Africa, on 28 September 1913, with Messrs. W. J. Dean and A. N. Smith, at the seventh hole, distance 272 yards, from his drive the ball of Mr. Edward Sladward struck a caddie (who was standing 150 yards away at the side of a tree just off the line of the fairway, and who was looking toward the tee) on the forehead just above the right

25

eye; the ball rebounded in a direct line 75 yards (distance measured). Beyond a slight abrasion of the skin, the caddie was not affected.

Most Courses Played

Up to 1953 Ralph Kennedy had played on over 3,615 different golf courses. He had an attested card of each one signed by an officer of the club or the professional. He had played in every state in the United States, every province in Canada, and twelve other countries: Bermuda, Cuba, Mexico, Panama, Colombia, Ecuador, Peru, Chile, Bolivia, and the British Isles. He visited Scotland in 1951 and played his 3,000th course over the Old Course, St. Andrews. Mr. Kennedy, of Scottish ancestry, was born on 16 June 1882, and started playing golf on 25 September 1910, but did not seriously attempt to make a record until after the First World War. He played the greatest number of different courses, namely, 160, in 1931, although in October 1935 he played thirty-one different courses in twelve days in the Minneapolis district. He played his 1,000th course on his fiftieth birthday, his 2,000th on his fifty-eighth birthday, his 2,800th on his sixty-eighth birthday, and his 3,000th on St. Andrews championship links. His favorite links are Winged Foot Golf Club, Pine Valley in New Jersey, Cypress Point in Del Monte, California, and Capielano at Vancouver in British Columbia. His favorite shots are the approach and putt. He made two holes in one, in August 1928, on the third hole, East Course, at the Winged Foot Golf Club, and the other in 1938 at Indian Hills Golf Club, Grand Rapids, Michigan.

J. H. Taylor played golf over fifty-five years, toured in many countries, and played on 1,000 golf courses. The late James Braid had played on 1,200 courses and designed or reconstructed approximately 500 courses.

Mr. A. O. Nicholson, president of the Farmers' and Merchants' State Bank, Shamrock, Texas, has kept a record of the 1,149 different courses he had completed up to March, 1961. He has had three holes in one.

Harry Vardon played on more than 1,000 different courses in many parts of the world, and Sandy Herd played on 1,200 different courses, some as far away as Mexico City.

Walter Hagen in about twenty-five years played on over 2,500 golf courses.

Jack Redmond, a noted trick-shot American golfer, claims that he has played on 2,800 courses in forty-one countries. Redmond has the unique record of playing thirty-six holes of golf at each stop on a business tour that carried him through India, Hawaii, South America, Australia, and Europe.

Longest Tournament

At the Fenway Country Club, New York, 22–25 September 1938, for a purse of $13,500, a tournament of over 108 holes was played on the basis of eighteen holes for two days and the low qualifiers to continue over thirty-six holes on the third day and thirty-six holes on the fourth day. This is the longest first-class tournament ever contested.

Longest Holes

The longest hole in the world is the seventeenth of 745 yards at the Black Mountain Club, North Carolina, opened in 1964. Cohanzick Country Club, New Jersey, and the Hot Springs Golf Club each have a hole 700 yards long. At Teyateyaneng, South Africa, they have one hole 619 yards and another which measures only 37 yards. The longest golf hole on a championship links in Great Britain is the sixth at Troon, 580 yards. The fifth hole on the Old Course, St. Andrews, is 576 yards long. The sixth at Carnoustie is 567 yards. The seventeenth at Westward Ho! is 551 yards long.

Long-Lived Golfers

The oldest golfer was Nathaniel Vickers who celebrated his 103rd birthday on Sunday, 9 October 1949, and died the following day. He was the oldest member of the United States Senior Golf Association and until 1942 he competed regularly in their events and won many trophies in the various age divisions. When one hundred years old he apologized for being able to play only nine holes a day. He was born in Moulton, Lincolnshire, and in 1885 went to the United States. He was an architect and designed many notable buildings, including some at Yale University. He was the architect for the Lady Chapel at St. Patrick's Cathedral, New York. He attributed his longevity and good health—excepting his hearing his faculties were little impaired—to heredity, contentment, and to taking it easy. He was never known to hurry.

A notable veteran who died in February 1963 was Willie Auchterlonie, age ninety-one. He was the last "home" Scot to win the British Open Championship—in 1893 at Prestwick. He founded the firm of D. and W. Auchterlonie, the famous St. Andrews clubmakers, and was an expert in fashioning handmade clubs. He had been professional to the Royal and Ancient Club since 1935. His duties included the firing of the miniature cannon as the R. and A. Club captain "played himself in" each year.

In his ninety-third year, the Reverend Harcourt Just had a daily round of six to ten holes at St. Andrews. In 1950, the Town Council gave him the "Courtesy of the Course," which excused the venerable minister from paying the yearly charge.

Mr. John Jeffrey and Mr. John Doleman, each at age of eighty-five, played an eighteen-hole match on Bruntsfield Links, August 1911.

Mr. T. E. Lewis, when seventy-eight years old, holed in one at the Mid-Surrey Golf Club's Course on 13 November 1909, playing his 138-yard shot with a brassie.

The tenth Earl of Wemyss played a round on his ninety-second birthday, in 1910, at Craigielaw. When eighty-seven the Earl was partnered by Harry Vardon in a match at Kilspindie, the golf course on his East Lothian estate at Gosford. The venerable Earl, after playing his ball, mounted a pony and rode to the next shot. He died 30 June 1914, in his ninety-sixth year. The eleventh Earl, also a keen golfer, succeeded to the title when over seventy. He used to say, "Everybody's father dies but my father."

Mr. F. L. Callender, age seventy-eight, in September 1932, played nine consecutive rounds in the Jubilee Vase, St. Andrews. He was defeated in the ninth, the final round, by 4 and 2. Callender's handicap was 12. This is the best known achievement of a septuagenarian in golf.

Longest Matches

W. R. Chamberlain, a retired farmer, and George New, a post-master at Chilton Foliat, on 1 August 1922, met at Littlecote, the nine-hole course of Sir Ernest Wills, and they agreed to play every Thursday afternoon over the course. This they did until Mr. New's sudden death on 13 January 1938. An accurate record of the matches was kept—a detailed record of each round, mentioning wind direction, playing conditions—and in the elaborate system nearly two million facts were recorded. They played 814 rounds, a total of 86,397 strokes, of which Mr. Chamberlain took 44,008 and Mr. New 42,371. Mr. New, therefore, was 1,637 strokes up. The last round was halved, a suitable end to such an unusual contest.

British Champions from Overseas

The British Amateur Championship was first won by a player from overseas in 1904 by Walter J. Travis, who was an Australian by birth but had become a naturalized citizen of the United States. He died in New York in 1927. Other golfers of other than British birth who have won the championship are Jesse Sweetser, 1926; R. T. Jones, 1930; W. Lawson Little, 1934-35; Robert

Sweeney, 1937; Charles Yates, 1938; William P. Turnesa, 1947; Frank R. Stranahan, 1948–50; Richard D. Chapman, 1951; Harvie Ward, 1952; J. W. Conrad, 1955; D. R. Beman, 1959; R. D. Davies, 1962; R. E. Cole, 1966; Bob Dickson, 1967. All these players are American except R. E. Cole of South Africa. Robert Sweeney learned and played most of his golf in England and served in the RAF before joining the USAF. In 1954 Douglas Bachli of Australia became the first competitor from that country to win the Amateur Championship. In 1966 R. E. Cole was the first South African to win the title.

The British Open Championship was first won by a player from overseas in 1907, by Arnaud Massy of France. The first American and the second player of other than British birth to win was Walter Hagen, 1922-24-28-29. Other overseas winners were Mr. R. T. Jones, 1926-27-30; Gene Sarazen, 1932; Denny Shute, 1933; Sam Snead, 1946; A. D. (Bobby) Locke, 1949-50-52-57; Ben Hogan, 1953; Peter Thomson, 1954-55-56-58-65; Gary Player, 1959-68; K. D. G. Nagel, 1960; Arnold Palmer, 1961-62; Tony Lema, 1964; J. Nicklaus, 1966-70. Three others entered from America have won the Open Championship; Jock Hutchison, 1921; Jim Barnes, 1925; and T. D. Armour, 1931; Hutchison and Armour are Scottish by birth, and Barnes was born in Cornwall. R. J. Charles, the 1963 winner, is the first New Zealander, and first left-handed player to win the Open Championship. The 1967 winner, Roberto de Vicenzo (Argentine) is the first South American to win the Open Championship.

Record Championship Winners

Mr. Robert Tyre Jones won the British Open Championship, 1926-27-30; British Amateur Championship, 1930; U.S. Open Championship, 1923-26-29-30; and the U.S. Amateur Championship, 1924-25-27-28-30—the most comprehensive series of victories in the world's championships. To win the four major golf championships of the world in one year, as Mr. Jones did in 1930, is an unparalleled feat which may never be repeated. Mr. Jones retired from competitive golf immediately after he won the U.S. Open, which was the last of the four championships. He was then twenty-eight years of age.

Mr. John Ball won the British Amateur Championship eight times, 1888-90-92-94-99-1907-10-12; the British Open, 1890; the Irish Open Amateur, 1893-94-99. Mr. H. H. Hilton won the British Amateur Championship four times, 1900-1-11-13; the British Open Championship twice, 1892-97; the Irish Open Championship four times, 1897-1900-1-2; and the American Amateur Championship, 1911.

Harry Vardon won the British Open Championship six times, 1896-98-99-1903-11-14; the German Open Championship, 1911; and the U.S. Open Championship, 1900. J. H. Taylor won the British Open Championship five times, 1894-95-1900-9-13; the French Championship twice, 1908-9; and the German Championship once, 1912.

James Braid won the British Open Championship five times, 1901-5-6-8-10.

Walter Hagen won the British Open Championship, 1922-24-28-29, and the U.S. Open Championship, 1914 and 1919. He won U.S.P.G.A. Championship in four consecutive years, 1924–27.

A. D. Locke won the British Open Championship, 1949-50-52-57; the South African Open Championship, 1935-37-38-39-40-46-50-51; and the South African Professional Championship, 1938-39-40-46-50-51.

Peter Thomson of Australia won the British Open Championship five times, 1954-55-56-58 and 1965.

Michael Bonallack (England) is the first player to win the British Amateur Championship in three consecutive years (1968–70). He has won it five times in all.

Bookmakers and Golf

Wagering on a heavy scale has been associated with golf from its earliest days, but the first time a bookmaker appeared at a golf tournament and shouted the odds was in 1898 in a professional tournament at Carnoustie. In 1927, at the British Open Championship at St. Andrews, a Glasgow bookmaker and two assistants mixed among the crowds following the players and shouting the odds. In the British Open Championship at Portrush, 1951, a bookmaker set up his stand during the qualifying rounds and shouted the odds. In 1934 various bookmakers' lists were promiscuously issued and publicly advertised, giving odds for the British Amateur and Open Championships, and representatives of different commission agents attended the two championships and touted for bets; but this was carried out individually, and odds were not publicly shouted. Since 1934 reputable bookmakers in London and the provinces annually bet to any sum on the Amateur and Open Championships.

Wagers, Curious and Large

In the Royal and Ancient Club minutes an entry on 3 November 1820 was made in the following terms: "Sir David Moncreiffe, Bart., of Moncreiffe, backs his life against the life of John Whyte-Melville, Esq., of Strathkinnes, for a new silver club as a present to the St. Andrews Golf Club, the price of the club to be paid by the survivor and the arms of the parties to be engraved on the club, and the present bet inscribed on it. No balls to be attached to it. In testimony of which this bet is subscribed by the parties thereto." Thirteen years later, Mr. Whyte-Melville, in a feeling and appropriate speech, expressed his deep regret at the lamented death of Sir Robert Moncreiffe, one of the most distinguished and zealous supporters of the club. Mr. Whyte-Melville, while lamenting the cause that led to it, had pleasure in fulfilling the duty imposed upon him by the bet, and accordingly delivered to the captain the silver putter. Whyte-Melville in 1883 was elected captain of the club a second time; he died in his eighty-sixth year in July 1883, before he could take office, and the captaincy remained vacant for a year. Old Whyte-Melville's portrait hangs in the Royal and Ancient clubhouse and is perhaps the finest and most distinguished picture in the smoking-room.

In 1766, the Honorable Company of Edinburgh Golfers, who then played at Leith Links, passed a resolution that "no match should be played for more than 100 merks on the day's play, or a guinea the round." A merk was worth 1s. 1½d., and the limit of 100 merks would be approximately £5 12s. 6d. in present-day money.

Heavy wagering is frequently associated with private or golfing society matches in which rich men are engaged, and rounds on which £1,000 depended are not unknown. Amateurs playing for £100 a round are not out of the way. When Bobby Jones won the four major championships in 1930 (the Amateur, the Open, the U.S. Amateur, and the U.S. Open) long odds had been laid against such a result by bookmakers, and extensive sums were paid out. In 1914 Francis Ouimet, who in the previous autumn had won the U.S. Open Championship after a triangular tie with Harry Vardon and Ted Ray, came to Great Britain with Jerome D. Travers, the holder of the U.S. amateur title, to compete in the British Amateur Championship at Sandwich. An American syndicate took a bet of £30,000 to £10,000 that one of the two United States champions would be the winner. It only took two rounds to decide the bet against the Americans. Ouimet was beaten by a quite unknown player, H. S. B. Tubbs, while Travers was defeated by Charles Palmer, who was fifty-six years of age at the time. This is believed to be the record golf wager as far as amount involved is concerned.

In 1907 Mr. John Ball, for a wager, undertook to go round Hoylake during a dense fog (1) under 90, (2) in two and a quarter hours, and (3) not to lose a ball. Mr. Ball played with a black ball, went round in 81, and also beat "time."

Ben Sayers, for a wager, played the eighteen holes of the Royal Burgess Society course in 4 each. Sayers was about to start against an American when his opponent asked him what he could do the course in. "Fours" replied Sayers, meaning 72, or an average of 4's for the round. A bet was made and the American then added, "Remember a 3 or a 5 is not a 4." There were eight 5's and two 3's on the Burgess course at the date Old Ben achieved his feat.

After a hole had been banged in one at Far Hills, New Jersey, one of the players offered to bet $10,000 to $1 that the occurrence would not be repeated at the hole during his lifetime.

Cross-country and freak matches have been fruitful of many wagers, and matches have been played between distinguished golfers using only a putting cleek against players carrying all their clubs. At Hoylake a match was fixed between a scratch golfer and a handicap-6 player. They played level, the handicap player having the right to say "Boo" three times on the round. He said "Boo" at the thirteenth hole. He won the match easily and had two "Boos" in hand, the scratch player, of course, being affected by always anticipating the "Boo."

A match was arranged on a south of England course for a considerable bet between a scratch player and a long-handicap man, play level, the scratch man to drink a whiskey and soda on each tee. On the sixteenth tee the scratch man, who had a hole lead, collapsed, and was not very well for some time afterward.

In November 1938, a proposed seventy-two-hole match received worldwide publicity. It was arranged between Brigadier-General Critchley and Alfred Perry against Harry Bentley and Henry Cotton, and the courses, Addington and Birkdale, were fixed. The first wager was £500 a side. Later Mr. Charles Moore, Southport, offered to back Mr. Bentley and Cotton for £2,000, making a total stake of £4,000. This was not accepted, and the match was not proceeded with.

In June 1950 Mr. Bryan Field, vice-president of the Delaware Park race course, who had not played golf for several years, accepted a wager that, without practice, he would not go round Pine Valley, rated one of the hardest courses in the world, in less than 300 shots. With borrowed clubs, he set off at 8 A.M. planning to finish in time for lunch. He started 7, 9, 4, 11, and when he got a 10 at the fifth, one of the most testing on the course, after putting three tee shots into the lake, it was obvious that he was well on the way to winning the bet. With an 11 at the eighth, another difficult hole, he reached the turn in 73. Coming home in

75, Mr. Field holed the course in 148 and won his wager with 152 strokes in hand. He took two hours fifty minutes to complete the round.

In 1952, Bobby Locke, the British Open Champion, played a round at Wentworth against any golfer in Britain. Cards costing 2s. 6d. each were taken out by 24,000 golfers. The challenge was to beat the local par by more than Locke beat the par of Wentworth: 1,641 competitors, including women, succeeded in "beating" the champion and each received a certificate signed by him. As a result of this challenge the British Golf Foundation benefited to the extent of £3,026, the proceeds from the sale of cards. A similar tournament was held in the United States and Canada when 87,094 golfers participated: 14,667 players bettered Ben Hogan's score under handicap. The fund benefited by $80,024. These tournaments are now annual events.

Record Number of Out-of-Bounds Shots

In the fifth round of the British Amateur Championship at Hoylake, 1910, Mr. Horace Hutchinson and Mr. Bernard Darwin tied. Playing the nineteenth hole Mr. Hutchinson sent his second and third shots out of bounds, but put his next clear. Mr. Darwin then played three shots out of bounds and retired from the match.

At the British Amateur Championship at Prestwick in 1934,

J. G. Montgomery, captain, Tantallon Golf Club, and an Englishman sent five balls out of bounds at the first hole. The railway from Ayr to Glasgow runs parallel to the entire length of the hole. The Englishman drove first, out of bounds. Montgomery followed. Both sent their seconds out of bounds. The Englishman sent his third shot, the fifth ball of the match, over the railway, and Montgomery, steadying himself, made sure that he did not go out of bounds. The Englishman conceded the hole without further play. These are records in any championship, five out-of-bound shots at one hole.

At this first hole, Prestwick, an almost unbelievable occurrence took place recorded by no less an authority than Bernard Darwin, as follows: "At Prestwick a friend of mine went out to play for a medal there feeling distinctly shattered by rather a late night. He put his tee shot onto the line, and the ball bounded back over the wall and onto the course. He thereupon put his second on the line, and this time the ball did better still, for it not only rebounded onto the green but ran into the hole. After this rather fortunate two he pulled himself together and won the competition."

In the British Open Championship at Muirfield, 1912, the U.S. Champion, M'Dermott, from the seventh tee, pulled three drives in succession out of bounds into Archerfield Wood, and was only saved from a similar disaster the fourth time by striking against the wall and rebounding onto the course.

In the British Open Championship, 1930, at Hoylake, A.

Tingey, Jr., cut three shots out of bounds at the first hole. Tingey had struck a long drive, and it was the shots to the green he sent out of bounds—penalty, stroke, and distance—so Tingey had run up to 8 to reach the green, and the hole cost him 11.

In the British Open Championship, 1938, at Sandwich, in the third round, when a hurricane was blowing, a competitor hit three drives out of bounds at the twelfth hole and eventually took 14 to the hole—equaling the third highest score for one hole ever recorded in the Open Championship.

The Feather, Gutta, and Rubber-Core Balls

The gutta-percha ball was introduced about 1848. Up to that year "featheries" were the only balls used for golf. Allan Robertson was one of the chief makers of the feather ball, and he had a disagreement with Tom Morris because "Old Tom" resolved to play with the new invention. The gutta ball, even in its primitive stage, quickly ousted the "feathery." The gutta passed through many stages, nicked, hand-hammered, and about 1900 it had reached a high state of perfection, the finest balls being sold at 12s. per dozen. The balls were economical in respect that the gutta could be melted and remade, and many professionals had their own molds and made their own golf balls. In 1901 the rubber-core ball was invented by C. Haskell, an American, and some of the new balls were tried in the British Amateur Championship at Hoylake in 1902. They gave little satisfaction, as they burst readily and were too lively on the putting green. A few weeks later, when the British Open Championship was decided, also at Hoylake, better examples of the rubber-core ball were available. Alex Herd played with a rubber-core and won the Open Championship. On the last day of the championship so great was the demand by professionals for the ball that fancy prices were paid for a single ball. The gutta ball was quickly superseded, and in 1903 the use of the rubber-core ball became general. The average score per round of the winners of the Open Championship for the years 1902–26 was 75.1, compared with an average score of 78.5 for the ten years prior to the introduction of the rubber-core ball. From 1902 the championship courses were gradually increased in length until they became approximately 500 yards longer than in the days of the gutta ball. From 1927 to 1949 the average winning score per round was 72.20, showing the continued improvement.

Balls in Strange Places

Balls have been accidentally driven into railway compartments of trains in motion and into vehicles passing or crossing golf courses. Such incidents are numerous in Scotland, where railway lines run alongside many links and public roads and cart tracks cut through the links. One example, playing at the John O'Gaunt

Club, Sutton, near Biggleswade (Bedfordshire), a member drove a ball which did not touch the ground until it reached London—over forty miles away. The ball landed in a vegetable lorry which was passing the golf course and fell out of a package of cabbages when it was unloaded at Covent Garden, London.

In the British Open Championship at Sandwich, 1949, Harry Bradshaw, Kilcroney, Dublin, led the qualifiers with 67, 72—139. In the first round of the championship he did 68 and led the field. In his second round he started with four 4s. At the fifth hole he drove into the rough and found his ball inside a beer bottle with the neck and shoulder broken off and four sharp points sticking up. The bottle was standing, and the ball had bounced into it. If he had treated the ball as in an unplayable lie, Bradshaw might have been involved in disqualification, so he decided to play it where it lay. With his blaster he smashed the bottle and sent the ball about 30 yards. The hole, a par-4, cost him 6. Bradshaw had taken about fifteen minutes to decide what he was to do. The flying splintered glass added to his discomfiture, and he said it was six more holes before he recovered his composure. Bradshaw took 77 to the round, his highest in the championship.

In the Universities match in 1904 C. H. Alison hit his approach to the last hole at Woking onto the clubhouse roof, where the ball remained. Not daunted, he secured a ladder, climbed onto the roof, played a splendid recovery, and halved the hole.

Playing at North Manchester Club in April 1963, Mr. Herbert Stead, at the thirteenth, found his ball in the rough inside a broken milk bottle. He exploded it out and finished the hole in one over par.

A member of Wildernesses Club, Kent, drove a ball from the first tee through a window of the professional's shop, where it ended up in a cup of tea which the professional was about to pick up. The teacup was undamaged, but the professional was slightly cut by broken glass from the window.

Playing to the second green at St. Andrews, Horace Hutchinson's ball landed on the shoulder of R. Kirk, the secretary of the St. Andrews Golf Club, and lodged in his breast pocket. In a match at the Cassiobury Park course of the West Herts Club one of the players made a drive from the tee on a misty day, and no one could tell where the ball went. After prolonged search in all directions the ball was ultimately discovered in the "turn up" of one of the legs of the player's trousers. He had carried it in this position from the tee to the hole. In 1908 a similar incident occurred at Bristol, and in December 1908 Lord Alverstone, in playing out of a bunker at one of the Birmingham Links, had his ball rebound into his jacket pocket. In August 1920, J. R. Hoise's tee shot finished by hitting a lady lightly, and the ball dropped into her sports-coat pocket. At Glasgow a ball rebounded off a stone and ran up the player's sleeve to the armpit. Even by extending the arm the ball was not dislodged, and it was only by unfastening the jacket that the ball was got out. In the £1,000 tournament at Brighton, 1939, E. S. Jones, Neath, playing his approach shot to the first hole, lodged the ball in a spectator's breast pocket. The spectator dropped the ball, and Jones incurred no penalty.

At Ladies Championship, Turnberry, 7 June 1937, Lady Eddis, Aldeburgh, lifted her ball out of casual water and dropped it. Lady Eddis pulled another club out of her bag to play the shot, but the ball was nowhere to be seen. An onlooker suggested it had not been dropped at all. The ball was discovered in a fold of Lady Eddis's jumper.

At Middleton, County Cork, in 1922, a member of the club, Mr. M'Evoy, drove from the third tee, the ball entering the ear of a donkey on the links. The donkey stood still, but when the players were within a few yards of the animal he took to his heels, tossed his head, and the ball came spinning to the ground.

On the Royal Dublin Course, 16 July 1936, in the Irish Open Championship, A. D. Locke, the South African, played his tee shot at the 100-yard twelfth hole, but the ball could not be found on arrival on the green. The marker removed the pin, and it was discovered that the ball had been entangled in the flag. It dropped near the edge of the hole, and Locke holed the short putt for a birdie-2.

While playing a round on the Geelong Golf Club course, Australia, Easter 1923, Captain Charteris topped his tee shot to the short second hole, which lies over a creek with deep and steep clay banks. His ball came to rest on the near slope of the creek bank. He elected to play the ball as it lay, and took his niblick. After the shot, the ball was nowhere to be seen. It was found embedded in a mass of gluey clay stuck fast to the face of the niblick. It could not be shaken off. It raised rather a pretty question. Charteris did what was afterward approved by the Royal and Ancient, cleaned the ball and dropped it behind without penalty.

At Duddingston, 22 April 1924, a ball became embedded on the back of a sheep. It was only after the sheep had been chased some distance that the ball was dislodged.

At Wallasey, 1925, Mr. W. C. Craigmile, coming up to his first drive, which he had topped into the rough, found his ball assailed by a swarm of angry wasps. The ball had rolled into the nest.

In October 1929, Blackmoor Golf Club, Bordon, Hants, driving from the first tee, a player holed out his ball in the chimney of a house some 120 yards distant and some 40 yards out of bounds on the right. The owner and his wife were sitting in front of the fire when they heard a rattle in the chimney, and were astonished to see a golf ball drop into the fire.

A good many years ago in the semifinal of the Yorkshire Professional Foursomes a ball that pitched close to the flag on a snow-covered green completely disappeared, but when the players were on the next tee it was discovered in a frozen lump of snow on a caddie's heel.

One of the most unusual shots on record was executed at Crawfordsville, Indiana, 26 August 1923, by Mrs. Blackford. After an approach shot had landed in a bird's nest, Mrs. Black-

ford climbed the tree in which the nest was situated, took a stance among the branches, and played a pitch shot onto the nearby green, from where she holed out in one putt and halved the hole.

The captain of Wick Golf Club, at the fifth hole on Reiss Course, after playing his drive, could not find his ball. He walked toward a hen which was sitting contentedly on the fairway. The hen scuttled away and revealed the missing ball.

In 1921 E. C. Davenport, honorary secretary of Tanamah Golf Club, Basrah, Iraq, played a shot at one hole in the date-palm belt. His ball appeared to lodge in the top of a date palm, and his Arab caddie climbed the tree in search. He found and threw down five balls, but Mr. Davenport's ball was not among them.

In July 1955 Mr. J. Lowrie, starter at the Eden Course, St. Andrews, witnessed a freak shot. A visitor drove from the first tee just as a northbound train was passing. He sliced the shot, and the ball disappeared through an open window of a passenger compartment. Almost immediately the ball emerged again, having been thrown back onto the fairway by a man in the compartment, who waved a greeting which presumably indicated that no one had been hurt.

Trick Shots

Joe Kirkwood, Australia, specialized in public exhibitions of trick and fancy shots. He played all kinds of strokes after calling them, and among his ordinary strokes nothing was more impressive than those hit for low flight. He played a full drive from the face of a wrist watch, and the toe of a spectator's shoe, full strokes at a suspended ball, and played for slice and pull at will, and exhibited his ambidexterity and played left-handed strokes with right-handed clubs. In his repertoire were holing six balls, stymied, and a full shot at a ball catching it as it descends; and hitting twelve balls in rapid succession, full shots, with his face turned away from the ball. In playing the last-named, Kirkwood placed the balls in a row, about 6 inches apart, and moved quickly along the line. Kirkwood, who was born in Australia, was for many years a resident of America.

Joe Ezar, an American professional, who specializes in trick shots, includes in his show a number of clowning acts with balls.

On 2 April 1894, a three-ball match was played over Musselburgh course between Messrs. Grant, Bowden, and Waggott, the clubmaker, the latter teeing on the face of a watch at each tee. He finished the round in 41, although the flags were not in the holes, the watch being undamaged in any way.

Young Tommy Morris drove off the face of a watch on St.

Andrews, and on the North Inch, Perth, in 1858, the local professional drove a ball off the face of a watch without injury to the face. It was a full drive. A similar feat has been frequently done.

At Westbrook, United States, in 1901, E. T. Knapp drove a ball off the top of a hen's egg. The egg was slightly dented on one end to afford a hold for the ball.

At Esther, 23 November 1931, George Ashdown, the club professional, played his tee shot for each of the eighteen holes in a match from a rubber tee strapped to the forehead of Miss Ena Shaw.

E. A. Forrest, a South African professional, in a music hall turn of trick golf shots, played blindfolded shots, one being from the ball teed on the chin of his recumbent partner.

Paul Hahn, an American trick specialist, can hit four balls with two clubs. Holding a club in each hand he hits two balls, hooking one and slicing the other with the same swing. Hahn has a repertoire of thirty trick shots. In 1955 he flew completely round the world, exhibiting in fourteen countries and on all five continents.

Speed of Golf Ball and Clubhead

The late Professor Tait estimated the initial velocity of a golf ball at 500 feet per second. This estimate, approximately 360 miles per hour, was negated by tests made in the United States. Gene Sarazen, British and U.S. Open Champion, 1932, made tests of actual ball speed in conjunction with the Packard Motor Company. It was estimated that the ball left the clubhead at the rate of 130 miles per hour and that the clubhead was traveling at 115 miles per hour. A high-speed car passed Sarazen at the moment of impact, and both the car and ball were timed. Tests carried out in which photoelectric measurement was used showed that the greatest speed of the clubhead at the moment of impact was 110.5 miles per hour.

Fatal and Other Accidents on the Links

The most astonishing and tragic death from a golf ball occurred in August 1914 at Wormit, Fifeshire. Private David Barnet was engaged with a detachment of the 4th Black Watch near the golf course, training before their departure for France to take part in the war. A ladies' competition was being played on the Wormit golf course, and a ball driven by one of the competitors struck Private Barnet on the temple. He was stunned by the blow but recovered and was able to walk with the assistance of his comrades to the house in which he was billeted. No serious consequences were feared, but within two days he lapsed into unconsciousness and died. A blood vessel in his head had been burst by the blow from the golf ball.

On 18 July 1881, on the North Course at Montrose, a player pulled his ball which struck a boy of about fourteen years of age on the back of the neck. The boy fell, rose, walked a few yards and again fell, and died in about five minutes.

In 1895 a boy was struck by a golf ball on the Portobello Links and killed. In July 1920, Joseph Casey, a twelve-year-old caddie, struck by a golf ball driven from a distance of 200 yards, was instantly killed on the links of the Yahnundasis Golf Club at Utica, and in 1927 a boy was killed by a golf ball at Leven. In 1928 a boy playing on a putting green in Wembley Council's Park was struck by a ball. He was knocked down and subsequently died from the effects of the blow. Years ago at East Wemyss in Fife, the local schoolmaster was hit on the knee with a feather ball, and his leg had to be amputated. At Given in July 1919 a player in swinging his club hit Mr. Robert Tait on the neck; the man fell unconscious and died shortly afterward. On 29 October 1927, at Foxhills, Los Angeles, Benjamin Wesley, an accountant, was accidentally killed while giving his twelve-year-old son a lesson in the game. After showing the boy the correct way to drive, the father handed the club to him and stepped to one side. The boy attempted to follow his father's instructions but missed the ball, and the club caught his father on the right temple with considerable force, the man dying almost instantly.

On a Toronto suburban golf course, Mr. Ted Abbott (age seventy-two), in October 1966, holed his tee shot at the eighth green—and died from a heart attack at the fourteenth.

At Wolstanton Golf Course, Newcastle-under-Lyme, 1934, John Bennett was passing along a private road which crosses the course when he was struck by a golf ball driven from the sixteenth tee. The ball was sliced and carried on the wind a distance of 130 yards; Bennett was struck in the face. Swelling set in, and septic poisoning spread to the skull. At the coroner's inquest the jury returned a verdict of "accidental death."

On 6 May 1933, Thomas William Inson, age fifteen, of Seven Kings, was accidentally struck on the head with a club while playing golf with two other boys of the brigade in camp at South Weald, near Brentford. He did not appear to be much hurt at the time but later complained of pain and giddiness, and died before the arrival of a doctor.

Edward M. Harrison, November 1951, while playing alone on the Inglewood Country Club, Seattle, apparently broke the shaft of his driver, and the split shaft pierced his groin. He tried to reach the clubhouse, but collapsed and bled to death 100 yards from the ninth tee, where the accident happened.

In the summer of 1963, Harold Kalles, of Toronto, Canada, died six days after his throat had been cut by a golf-club shaft, which broke against a tree as he was trying to play out of a bunker.

On 4 May 1936, C. H. Short, Cranford, traveling between Boston Manor and Osterley on the Piccadilly Railway, was reading his paper when he was struck on the head by a ball from Wyke Green Golf Club, which adjoins the line. Short fell forward with blood streaming from his face. He collapsed at Osterley station and was removed to Hounslow Hospital in the ambulance. He recovered after treatment.

At Jacksonville, Florida, 18 March 1952, two women golfers were instantly killed when hit simultaneously by the whirling propeller of a navy fighter plane. They were playing together when the plane, with a dead engine and coming in against the wind, out of control, hit them from behind. The propeller hurled one body 35 feet and the other 65 feet. The pilot making a test flight from the naval air station which adjoins the golf course, stepped out of the burning plane and did not know for some seconds that the plane had killed the women. A Negro caddie for the victims said he was walking behind the women along the edge of the fairway and did not see the plane until it was a few yards from the golfers. He yelled, but the plane hit the players within a second or two. A witness to the accident said, "I went through two world wars, but never saw anything so ghastly. The propeller hit both women at the same instant."

In 1956 Philip Walker, sixteen, San Diego, California, was killed by a golf club. He was hit on the head by the follow-through of a friend who was practicing with him at a range.

In September 1956, Myrl G. Hanmore, aged fifty, died from an accident at the Riviera Country Club, Los Angeles, apparently caused when he lost control of a golf car on a steep incline and was crushed between the vehicle he was driving and one he was towing from the first tee to a storage barn.

In June 1919, at Deauville, Mr. Jimmy de Rothschild, who was wearing a monocle, was struck on the monocle, and the eye was so badly damaged that it had to be removed. Mr. de Rothschild, art connoisseur, farmer, racehorse owner and former Liberal M.P., died in May 1957, at the age of seventy-eight and left more than £11 million.

In November 1923 Professor Schuster, the well-known scientist, also had his eye damaged when struck by a golf ball. In June 1919, at Killermont, a club slipped out of the grasp of the player and hit a spectator on the jaw. The man's jaw was broken. On a Welsh course a player had played a shot out of a bunker and jumped up to see the result, when he was hit on the head by a ball driven from behind. He felt no ill effects at the moment, except a slight smarting of the eyes, but within a week he was totally blind.

At Chiselhurst, in 1923, Mr. Wakasugi, a secretary of the Japanese Embassy in London, hit a guide post; and the ball, rebounding, struck him on the forehead and rendered him unconscious. An ugly wound had to be stitched. While Karl Klinger was playing at Victoria Park, Brisbane, his drive hit a telegraph pole. The ball rebounded and fell behind him. Under the local rule, he dropped another and played it. It also rebounded, hit Klinger, fracturing his nose, and he dropped unconscious.

At Harrogate in 1926 a competitor in an open tournament, excited because he had holed a 20-yard putt on the eighteenth green, flung his club into the air, and it came down on his partner's head, knocking him temporarily unconscious. After treatment at the clubhouse the injured man was able to go home.

An unusual tragedy occurred on the West Herts Links in 1923. Mr. H. J. Osborne, playing in a foursome, was standing under an elm tree when a branch fell and killed him. Mrs. Osborne, who partnered her husband, had her skull fractured, and the two other players in the foursome just succeeded in getting clear of the falling branch.

In 1927 a curious accident befell a member of the audience at the Vaudeville Theatre, London. While Mr. Norman Griffin was swinging a golf club in his sketch, "I do look a lad in plus-fours," the iron head flew into the auditorium. It struck the circle and fell upon the head of an Eton schoolboy named Tate who was one of a party of four, including his father, mother, and brother. Tate received a cut on the forehead and had to be taken to Charing Cross Hospital for the wound to be dressed. He returned in about twenty minutes and expressed sorrow that he had lost a part of the performance.

In the thirty-six-hole final of the Yorkshire £750 Professional Tournament, 1935, at Sand Moor, T. H. Cotton, against Percy Alliss, was dormie-3. Cotton played his second shot, and the ball soared over the green, struck a spectator on the forehead, and rebounded. The man fell unconscious, and the ball finished on the green instead of going out of bounds. Cotton halved the hole, which gave him a victory of three up and two to play.

At Philadelphia, August 1939, James B. McFarland, twenty-seven-year-old amateur golfer, was convicted of involuntary manslaughter by causing the death of a caddie. McFarland said: "After a bad shot I swung my club in disgust, too forcibly. The club slipped out of my hands and hit and killed the caddie, who was 15 feet away."

In 1938, at Soangetaha Country Club, Galesburg, Illinois, David Rutledge, a caddie, age fifteen, was stung by a bee and became blind. He sued the club, and he was awarded the maximum compensation of $2400 plus $24 a month for life and $336 for medical fees.

A. W. Good at Lewes, in swinging at his second shot at the sixth hole, overbalanced and somersaulted into a sheep trough which was full of water.

A Texan, Mr. Moody Weaver, used such force in a practice swing that he broke his leg in two places, above the knee and above the ankle.

Golf Balls Killing Animals and Fish, and Incidents with Animals

The most astounding fatality to an animal caused by a golf ball occurred at St. Margaret's-at-Cliffe Golf Club, Kent, on 13 June 1934, when W. J. Robinson, the professional, killed a cow with his tee shot to the eighteenth hole. The eighteenth is a short hole,

and Robinson used a No. 2 iron. The cow was standing in the fairway about 100 yards from the tee, and the ball struck her on the back of the head. She fell like a log, but staggered to her feet and walked about 50 yards before dropping again. When the players reached her she was dead. The incident was fully corroborated by Mr. T. D. Southgate, honorary secretary of the club.

As Mrs. Molly Whitaker played from a bunker at Beachwood Course, Natal, South Africa, a large monkey leaped from a bush and clutched her round the neck. A caddie drove it off by clipping it with an iron club.

J. W. Perret of Ystrad Mynach, playing with Charles R. Halliday of Ralston in the qualifying rounds of the Society of One-Armed Golfers' Championship over the Darley Course, Troon, on 27 August 1935, killed two gulls at successive holes with his second shots. The "deadly" shots were at the first and second holes.

In 1906, in the Border Championship at Hawick, a gull and a weasel were killed by balls during the afternoon's play.

A golfer at Newark in May 1907 drove the ball into the river. The ball struck a 2-lb. trout and killed it.

Playing over the Killarney Course, June 1957, a golfer sliced his ball into one of the lakes and knocked out a trout rising to catch a fly. His friend waded into the water to get the ball—and the trout.

In 1921, at Kettering, a drive, badly skied, killed a sparrow-hawk.

In 1921 at the Broxbourne Golf Club, Herts, a member drove off from the third tee simultaneously with the rise of a covey of partridges, one of which was struck by the ball and killed. Here the question arose as to the ownership of the bird, and had the golfer a game license. At all events it was a shot that provided a good dinner.

On 30 September 1929, when the Reverend Davies Jones, in a match on Bala Golf Course, took his stroke for a ball that had fallen at the mouth of a rabbit hole, a rabbit appeared and was killed by the mashie.

A surfeit of "birdies" distracted an Australian golfer, Mr. S. Ely, a stationmaster from Leongatha, Victoria. Crows picked up two of his golf balls on the fifth hole. About to drive on at the seventh tee, he "sliced" badly when a kookaburra laughed harshly. The bird repeated its noise as he was about to play his third shot—also sliced. Finally, when Mr. Ely got his ball on the green, the kookaburra swooped down, picked up the ball, and flew off with it. This time it didn't laugh. Nor did Mr. Ely.

At Worthing, on 16 March 1952, two brothers, Keith and Malcolm Clayton, were partnered in a foursome. There was heavy fog, and when at the first tee Keith drove, a flock of seagulls rose from the fairway. The ball struck one and killed it. At the fifteenth hole, when Malcolm played the second shot, once again a flock of seagulls rose, and one was struck and killed. The game was a two-ball, and the same ball was used throughout the round.

A little pond beside the sixth fairway on the Fort Polk, Louisiana, course contains an unusual hazard, and golfers are warned that they should not wade into it in search of a wayward drive. It is the home of an alligator of unpredictable temper.

Killed and Struck by Lightning on the Links

Players when overtaken by thunderstorms should note that the elevation of golf clubs above one's normal height is dangerous. Steel shafts and the ribs in large golf umbrellas may attract lightning. It is safer to lay down the golf clubs and seek shelter.

Scientists advise that the safest thing to do when caught in a severe thunderstorm is to lie flat on the ground, for the highest point in an otherwise flat surface is liable to be struck. Avoid isolated trees, wire fences, small, exposed, and isolated shelters. Seek a grove of trees, a dense wood, a cave, a depression in the ground.

At the Ladies' Championship, Gleneagles, 1933, there were violent storms, and an official announcement was made advising competitors, in the event of a thunderstorm, to throw their clubs down and leave them until the storm passed over. The Royal and Ancient and the USGA in the New Rules of Golf, 1 January 1952 (Rule 37-6), provide for discontinuance of play. Unfortunately, numerous players, caddies, and greenkeepers have been killed by lightning. The following are among the more remarkable:

1932: On Maidenhead Golf Course, Peter Kelly, age seventy-two, a director of Booths' Distilleries, and Horace Walter James Miles, age fifteen, his caddie, were killed by lightning. G. H.

Edwards, who was playing Kelly, was burnt in the face, hands, and right side. The golfers were sheltering under a tree. The umbrella which Kelly held was burned and twisted; and while none of the steel-shafted clubs was damaged, the bottom of the caddie's bag was torn out. This may suggest that the lightning found its way to earth partly through the medium of the steel. At the inquest, medical evidence disclosed that the hair on Mr. Kelly's head and his beard were burnt, and there were extensive burns on the neck, chest, back, both arms, and right leg. There was also a burn on the front of the left shin. The caddie's hair was burnt off the back of the head down to the scalp. There were extensive burns on the left side and front of the neck, left shoulder, left arm, and the left chest back and front. The effect of the burns in both cases was instantaneous death.

1937: At Whittlesea, near Queenstown, South Africa, a native caddie boy was killed. The lightning traveled twice round the lad's body before grounding itself. A 3-penny piece the boy had in his mouth burned a hole through his tongue. At the time the sky was cloudless.

1952: On the Island Club Course, Singapore, D. P. Gilroy, an official of the Shell Oil Company and his Chinese caddie were killed when the hut in which they were sheltering was struck by lightning.

1953: At Pittsburgh Field Club Miss Pat Hinkel, age twenty, was receiving a lesson from the local professional when a storm broke and the professional raised his golf umbrella to protect his pupil. This attracted lightning; pupil and professional were rendered unconscious and removed to a hospital, where Miss Hinkel died. The professional, Pete Snead, brother of Sam Snead, was discharged after several days.

1954: At South Shore Country Club, near Rockland, Massachusetts, in July, Richard Clifford was struck by lightning and killed. The flash also knocked down John D. Haughey, Jr., and a caddie, who were sheltering from heavy rain under trees which the lightning struck.

1957: On 16 June at Scranton Country Club, Pennsylvania, three golfers were killed and another player and two caddies were injured when lightning cracked down onto the sixteenth tee while the golfing party was sheltering under a tree. On 22 June, at Lexington Country Club, Kentucky, lightning struck an electric caddy cart in which three golfers were hurrying to the clubhouse. One man was killed, and the other two were injured.

1963: A Clydebank boy golfer, Thomas Friel, age sixteen, was killed by lightning while sheltering in a tree on Dalmuir Golf Course, near Glasgow, on 2 August.

1964: John White, the Scotland and Tottenham Hotspur football star, was killed by lightning on Crews Hill Golf Course, Enfield, Middlesex, on 21 July. He was playing alone and had sheltered under an oak tree beside the first fairway.

1966: A bolt of lightning, on 12 July, struck the chimney of the Eberhart-Pietro clubhouse at Mishawaka, Indiana. Lewis M. Sheddon, age fifty-two, a native of Wishaw, Scotland, about to step through the doorway of the clubhouse, was struck by falling bricks. He died a half hour later.

1968: Hector McLeod of Edinburgh was killed by lightning while sheltering under a tree with three other players at Ratho Golf Course, near Edinburgh. All four were knocked to the ground.

Lightning—Official Rules for Discontinuing Play

The Rules of Golf (Rule 37-6) permit a player to discontinue play without penalty if he considers that there be danger from lightning.

The United States Golf Association recommends the following guide, compiled by the National Bureau of Standards, for personal safety during thunderstorms:

(a) Do not go out of doors or remain out during thunderstorms unless it is necessary. Stay inside of a building where it is dry, preferably away from fireplaces, stoves, and other metal objects.
(b) If there is any choice of shelter, choose in the following order:
   1. Large metal or metal-frame buildings,
   2. Dwellings or other buildings which are protected against lightning,
   3. Large unprotected buildings,
   4. Small unprotected buildings.

(c) If remaining out of doors is unavoidable, keep away from:
1. Small sheds and shelters if in an exposed location,
2. Isolated trees,
3. Wire fences,
4. Hilltops and wide open spaces.
(d) Seek shelter in:
1. A cave,
2. A depression in the ground,
3. A deep valley or canyon,
4. The foot of a steep or overhanging cliff,
5. Dense woods,
6. A grove of trees.

NOTE: Raising golf clubs or umbrellas above the head is dangerous.

Birds and Animals Interfering with Golf Balls and Attacking Players

Crows, ravens, hawks, and seagulls frequently carry off golf balls, sometimes dropping the ball actually on the green, and it is a common incident for a cow to swallow a golf ball. A plague of crows on the Royal Liverpool course at Hoylake are addicted to golf balls—they stole twenty-six in one day, selecting only new balls. It was suggested that members should carry shotguns as a fifteenth club.

A match was approaching a hole in a rather low-lying inland

course, when one of the players made a crisp chip from about 30 yards from the hole. The ball trickled slowly across the green and eventually disappeared into the hole. After a momentary pause the ball was suddenly ejected onto the green, and out jumped a large frog.

In 1921 on the course at Kirkfield, Ontario, P. M'Gregor and H. Dowie were all square going to the home hole in the final, and when they reached the green M'Gregor needed to hole a long putt to win the match. He played the ball to the lip of the hole. It seemed to have stopped, when a large grasshopper landed squarely on the ball and caused it to drop into the hole and decide the match in favor of M'Gregor.

A young bullock, which was one of a herd that grazed on land adjoining the Headingley (Leeds) golf course, was seen to be losing weight. When its owner, farmer George Dalby, had it slaughtered, he was astonished to find fifty-six golf balls in its stomach.

In the summer of 1963, Mr. S. C. King had a good drive to the tenth hole at the Royal Guernsey Club. His partner, Mr. R. W. Clark, was in the rough, and Mr. King helped him to search. Returning to his ball, he found a cow eating it. Next day, at the same hole, the positions were reversed, and King was in the rough. Clark placed his woollen hat over his ball, remarking, "I'll make sure the cow doesn't eat mine." On his return he found the cow thoroughly enjoying his hat; nothing was left but the pom-pom.

At Callander, Perthshire, a crow carried a golf ball from the Callander course to a hillside a mile distant. The most extraordinary record of a bird appropriating golf balls was in 1925, on the Aberdare Valley golf course. Three golfers saw a raven fly off with one of the balls on the green. Two holes farther on another ball was stolen by the same bird, which followed the golfers and flew off with three more balls, one of which, however, it dropped while in flight. When the golfers returned they learned that three balls had also been stolen from two players following them—the only other people on the course. That made eight balls stolen by the raven. On the Bass Rock, which is near North Berwick, golf balls have been observed in nests of solan geese. In a badger's "sett" twelve golf balls were found when the badger was dug out, and a rat has been observed pushing a golf ball in front of him in the same way as the rodent rolls an egg toward his nest.

Squirrels are known to appropriate golf balls, and in one squirrel's nest over a dozen have been found; no doubt most of them would be lost balls, and gathered by the squirrel. An instance, however, is recorded of a squirrel boldly stealing a ball. It occurred in 1923 on the Rivermead Links, Ottawa. Mr. Arnold W. Duclos, K.C., Ottawa, was playing the thirteenth, which is a short hole between trees, when the ball hit a branch and fell short of the green. Thereupon a squirrel, which was in the tree, ran down, lifted the ball, and ran away with it to its nest, notwithstanding the players endeavoring to make him drop it.

In a wood adjoining the municipal links, Winnipeg, workmen

removing timber discovered in a cavity formed by the timbers, arranged in a most methodical manner, a large collection of golf balls of all kinds. There were 250 balls nicely arranged in lines, and packed in moss. A professor of natural history came to the conclusion that the balls had been carried from the golf course to the cache by a little animal called a gopher. The naturalist considered that the gopher, thinking the balls were eggs, had stored them for food against the winter.

The greenkeeper, St. Michael's Club, Sydney, watched crows dropping golf balls from a height onto rocks, obviously with the intention of smashing them expecting food to be inside. After the crows had failed he watched them push the balls under a bush. He marked the bush and found a nest of 144 balls.

In 1928 two members of the Burton-on-Trent Golf Club were playing in the autumn singles, when one of them, Mr. A. Whedden, had a curious experience. A lamb picked up the ball in its mouth, and, before either player could interfere, dropped it into the hole, despite the fact that the flagstick was still there.

At Cairo in 1903, a player pulled into the rough, and on going to look for his ball he saw a snake suddenly emerging from a patch of grass; it seized the ball in its jaws and disappeared down a hole. The snake probably mistook the ball for an egg.

In 1928 two players at the fifteenth hole Old Course, Fanling, saw a small animal lying on the green. One player put his second onto the green. The animal, a fox, picked up the ball and carried it to the back of the bank, where it was subsequently found.

Foxes have been seen often on this course, and balls well bitten by them have been found.

At Dungannon Golf Links, County Tyrone, October 1936, a ram attacked two players on the seventh green. They tried to beat it off with their clubs but were unsuccessful. They then took cover behind a tree, but the ram again attacked them, and they decided that discretion was the better part of valor and gave up their game.

At lonely points on Scottish golf courses lapwings, or peewits as they are called in Scotland, have been known to attack players who may have wandered into the rough in search of a ball which has gone off the line. If the young peewits are just out and creeping about the tufts of grass the parent birds swoop fiercely at the intruders, who beat them away by waving their clubs.

At Highpost Golf Club, Salisbury, Wiltshire, August 1952, E. I. Hobden and D. Petts, playing an evening round, were attacked by a falcon. The bird attacked again and again, striking at the players' eyes. Mr. Hobden made an effective swipe and killed the attacking bird.

On golf courses in Kenya lions are occasionally encountered, wolves have been seen, and on courses in India many different kinds of wild animals are observed.

On a golf course in Arizona, in 1951, Dr. H. J. Morland was lining up his putt for a birdie-4 on the fourth hole. He struck the ball, but as it rolled toward the hole it suddenly stopped dead.

71

On examining the ball the doctor found an earthworm entwined round it. The worm must have come out of the green and been struck by the ball, which it encircled and stopped short of the hole.

At Royal Mid-Surrey during the Star Tournament in 1945, a very young and frightened grouse was imprisoned by the crowd which encircled one of the greens. J. Shoesmith, who won the tournament, had put his ball on the lip of the hole and the bird, running round and round flapping its wings, fanned the ball into the hole.

At Waimairi Golf Club, New Zealand, a two-year-old tomcat, Smoky by name, owned by the greenkeeper, used to lie on the ground near the implement shed and had a habit of chasing balls when they reached the ground. There were many incidents of Smoky deflecting short putts into the hole and a few others where he stopped good putts from going down. He constituted something extra special in the wide category covered by the technical term "rub of the green."

In August 1953, dense swarms of flying ants drove golfers off the Jubilee and New Courses at St. Andrews. The holes affected most were the eighth, ninth, tenth, and eleventh of the New Course, the insects apparently preferring the sand areas around bunkers and teeing grounds.

Armless, One-armed, Legless, and Ambidextrous Players

In September 1933, at Royal Burgess Golfing Society of Edinburgh, the first championship for one-armed golfers was held. There were 43 entries, and 37 of the competitors had lost an arm in the 1914–18 war. Play was over two rounds, and the championship was won by W. E. Thomson, Eastwood, Glasgow, with a score of 169 (82 and 87) for two rounds. The Royal Burgess Course was 6,300 yards long. Thomson drove the last green, 260 yards. The championship and an international match are played annually.

In the Boys' Amateur Championship, 1923, at Dunbar, and in 1949 at St. Andrews, there were competitors with one arm. The competitor in 1949, R. P. Reid, Cupar, Fife, who lost his arm working a machine in a butcher's shop, got through to the third round.

Thomas P. M'Auliffe, formerly a caddie at Buffalo, is an armless golfer. M'Auliffe holds the club handle between his right shoulder and cheek. He has gone round the Buffalo Country Club links in 108. Major Frank B. Edwards, late of the Second Canadian Mounted Rifles, who had both his arms blown off below the elbow in the fighting on the Somme in October 1915, can write, swim, play billiards, and golf. His golf clubs were specially made. Robert Topp of Macduff is another armless golfer.

Mr. D. R. S. Bader, a member of North Hants Golf Club, in spite of the handicap of two artificial legs, plays round that course in a shorter time than most, playing his strokes without the use of stick or crutch, and has figured as a winner of club events.

Group Captain Bader, who lost both legs in a flying accident prior to the 1939–45 war, took part in golf competitions and reached a single figure handicap in spite of his disability.

At Joliet Country Club, a one-armed golfer named D. R. Anderson drove a ball 300 yards.

Playing in a four-ball match at Wooden Bridge, County Wicklow, in 1926 Mr. J. S. Potter, honorary secretary of the club, holed the fourth hole, 110 yards, in one stroke. Mr. Potter uses his right arm only. His left arm was injured in the First World War.

Being left-handed but playing golf right-handed is prevalent, and for a man to throw with his left hand and play golf right-handed is considered an advantage for Mr. Bobby Jones, Mr. Jesse Sweetser, Walter Hagen, Jim Barnes, and Joe Kirkwood, eminent golfers who are ambidextrous.

In a practice round for the British Open Championship in July 1927, at St. Andrews, Mr. Len Nettlefold and Joe Kirkwood changed sets of clubs at the ninth hole. Nettlefold is a left-handed golfer and Kirkwood right-handed. They played the last nine, Kirkwood with the left-handed clubs and Nettlefold with the right-handed clubs.

74

There are a considerable number of ambidextrous players. Mr. Robert Smith, of Sydney, could play equally well with left- or right-hand clubs, and in 1909 he played a round "left hand" against "right hand," wagers being laid. Victor East is another noted ambidextrous player. Harry Vardon, when he was at Ganton, got tired of giving impossible odds to his members and beating them, so he collected a set of left-handed clubs and, rating himself at scratch, conceded the handicap odds to them. He won with the same monotonous regularity.

Ernest Jones, who was professional at the Chislehurst Club, was badly wounded in the war in France in 1916, and his right leg had to be amputated below the knee. With remarkable fortitude, however, he persevered with the game, and before the end of the year he went round the Clacton course, balanced on his one leg, in 72. Jones later settled in the United States, where he built fame and fortune as a golf teacher.

Major Alexander Macdonald Fraser, well-known Edinburgh golfer, has had the distinction of holding two handicaps simultaneously in the same club—one when he plays left-handed and the other for his right-handed play. In medal competitions he had to state before teeing up which method he would use. Major Fraser, who has played for the Scottish club secretaries against the English, derives his ambidexterity from his shinny days in the Highlands.

Cross-Country Matches

The longest cross-country or "hole" played in the British Isles was in 1913 from Linton Park near Maidstone to Littlestone Links, a distance as the cow flies of 26 miles, but in actual play 35 miles. The wager was modest, £5 that the player did not hole out under 2,000 shots. T. H. Ovler (who died in 1941, age ninety-one) accepted the bet, and he did "the hole" in 1,087 strokes. He occupied three days in the play, seventeen balls were lost in rivers, woods, and scrub, and sixty-two balls were lifted out of impossible lies, off railway lines and out of backwaters. A condition of the bet was that the ball had to be played where it lay, or lifted under penalty.

Two members of Radyr (Cardiff) Golf Club played a cross-country golf game covering some 28 miles in November 1963. Starting at 8 A.M. on Saturday the 23d on the first tee of Radyr Club, they finished at 6:40 A.M. on Sunday the 24th, on the eighteenth green of Royal Porthcawl Club. Messrs. Keith Halewood (handicap 4) and Ben Roberts (2) played one ball with alternate shots, using one wooden club and three irons. Making wide detours to avoid marshes, woods, etc., they played 707 shots, and 51 balls were lost (penalty two strokes) in 19 hours, 55 minutes' playing time. They slept out on the course on the night of the 23d, and completed the last three miles in darkness, along the roadway, with the aid of car headlights. They were accompanied all the way by at least one caddie and marker. A television camera man followed the game.

The longest cross-country match in America was on 5 June 1929, when the brothers Clyde and Harold McWhirter played between Spartanburg and Union, South Carolina, a distance of 36¾ miles. They started at 5:18 A.M. Their time, 13 hours 4 minutes. Clyde took 780 shots and Harold 825. They lost twenty-two balls between them, and used eight caddies; four rode in the official's car to rest, alternating with four others out in front watching balls. Each ball was teed up. The time by the Americans is astonishing; they traveled at the rate of approximately 3 miles per hour.

In 1830 the Gold Medal winner of the Royal and Ancient backed himself for 10 sovereigns to drive from the first hole at St. Andrews to the toll bar at Cupar, distance 9 miles, in 200 teed shots. He won easily.

In 1848 two Edinburgh golfers played a match from Bruntsfield Links to the top of Arthur's Seat—an eminence overlooking the Scottish capital, 822 feet above sea level. Other occurrences are recorded in the minutes of the Royal Burgess Golfing Society as follows: "Bruntsfield Links, 13th May 1815. Mr. Scott betted one guinea with Mr. Dowall that he would drive a ball from the Golf House over Arthur's Seat, at 45 strokes. Mr. Scott lost. Mr. Brown betted with Mr. Spalding one gallon of whisky that he would drive a ball over Arthur's Seat on the terms and at the same number of strokes as the above bet. Mr. Spalding lost, as Mr. Brown drove his ball in 44 strokes."

In 1880 Willie Campbell and Mr. B. Hall Blyth played from Point Garry, North Berwick, to the High Hole at Gullane. Willie Campbell took the shore route playing over North Berwick, Archerfield, and the land which ultimately became Muirfield, and Mr. Hall Blyth played inland through Dirleton. Mr. Hall Blyth, who was a civil engineer by profession and a man of giant build, selected the longer but much simpler course and won very easily, Campbell getting among the rocks. The distance was 6 miles.

On a winter's day in 1898, Freddie Tait backed himself to play a gutta ball in forty teed shots from St. George's Clubhouse, Sandwich, to the Cinque Ports Club, Deal. He was to hole out by hitting any part of the Deal clubhouse. The distance as the crow flies was 3 miles. The redoubtable Tait holed out with his thirty-second shot, and so effectively that the ball went through a window.

On 3 December 1920, Mr. P. Rupert Phillips and Mr. W. Raymond Thomas teed up on the first tee of the Radyr Golf Club and played to the last hole at Southerndown. The distance as the crow flies is 15½ miles, but circumventing swamps, woods, and plough, they covered approximately 20 miles. They holed out on 5 December. The wager was that they would not do the "hole" in 1,000 strokes. They holed out at their 608th stroke. They carried large ordnance maps.

In 1900 three members of the Hackensack, New Jersey, club played a game of 4½ hours over an extemporized course 6 miles long, which stretched from Hackensack to Paterson. Despite rain,

cornfields, and wide streams, the three golfers—J. W. Hauleebeck, Dr. E. R. Pfaare, and Eugene Crassons—completed the round, the first- and the last-named taking 305 strokes each, and Dr. Pfaare 327 strokes. The players used only two clubs, the mashie and the cleek.

In 1919 a golfer drove a ball from Piccadilly Circus and proceeding via the Strand, Fleet Street, and Ludgate Hill, "holed out" at the Royal Exchange, London. The player drove off at 8 A.M. on a Sunday, a time when the usually thronged thoroughfares were deserted.

On 23 April 1939, Richard Sutton, a London stockbroker, played from Tower Bridge, London, to White's Club, St. James's Street, in 142 strokes. The bet was he would not do "the course" under 200 shots. Sutton used a putter, crossed the Thames at Southwark Bridge, and hit the ball short distances to keep out of trouble.

On 19 November 1932, R. S. Little and K. G. Sherriff, students at St. Andrews University, played a cross-country match from Ceres, an inland Fifeshire village, to the home hole at St. Andrews. The conditions: each was to use one club, they were to tee up at each shot, and to hole out in less than 300 strokes. The distance was 9 miles, and they took eight hours. Mr. Little holed out in 236 strokes and Mr. Sherriff in 238 strokes.

Golfers produced the most original event in Ireland's three-week national festival of An Tostal, 1953—a cross-country competition with an advertised £1,000,000 for the man who could hole out in one. The 150 golfers drove off from the first tee at

Kildate Club to hole out eventually on the eighteenth green 5 miles away on the nearby Curragh Course, a distance of 8,800 yards. The unusual hazards to be negotiated included the main Dublin-Cork railway line and highway, the Curragh Racecourse, hoofprints left by Irish Thoroughbred racehorses out exercising on the plains from nearby stables, army tank tracks, and about 150 telephone lines. The Golden Ball Trophy, which is played for annually—a standard-size golf ball in gold, mounted on a black marble pillar beside the silver figure of a golfer on a green marble base, designed by Captain Maurice Cogan, Army GHQ, Dublin—was for the best gross. And it went to one of the longest hitters in international golf today—Amateur Champion, Irish Internationalist, and British Walker Cup player Joe Carr, with the remarkable score of 52—two better than G. N. Hogarty (Howth), the runner-up.

Golf Matches Against Other Sports

Mr. H. H. Hilton and Mr. Percy Ashworth, many times racket champion, contested a driving match, the former driving a golf ball with a driver, and the latter a racket ball with a racket. Best distances: Against breeze, golfer 182 yards, racket player 125 yards; down wind, golfer 230 yards, racket player 140 yards. Afterward Mr. Ashworth hit a golf ball with the racket and got a greater distance than with the racket ball, but was still a long way behind the ball driven by Mr. Hilton.

In 1913, at Wellington, Shropshire, a match between a golfer and a fisherman casting a 2½ oz. weight was played. The golfer, Mr. Rupert May, took 87; the fisherman, Mr. J. J. D. Mackinlay, required 102. The fisherman's difficulty was in his short casts. His longest cast, 105 yards, was within 12 yards of the world's record, held by a French angler, Decautelle. When within a rod's length of a hole he ran the weight to the rod end and dropped into the hole. Five times he broke his line, and was allowed another shot without penalty.

In December 1913 Mr. F. M. A. Webster, of the London Athletic Club, and Miss Dora Roberts, with javelins, played a match with Harry Vardon and Mrs. Gordon Robertson, who used the regulation clubs and golf balls. The golfers conceded two-thirds in the matter of distance, and they won by five up and four to play in a contest of eighteen holes. The javelin throwers had a mark of two feet square in which to "hole out" while the golfers had to get their ball into the ordinary golf hole. Mr. Webster's best throw was one of 160 feet.

Several matches have taken place between a golfer on the one side and an archer on the other. The wielder of the bow and arrow has nearly always proved the victor. In 1953 at Kirkhill Golf Course, Lanarkshire, five archers beat six golfers by two games to one. There were two special rules for the match: when an archer's arrow landed 6 feet from the hole or the golfer's ball 3 feet from the hole, they were counted as holed. When the arrows landed in bunkers or in the rough, archers lifted their arrow and added a stroke. The sixth archer in this match called off, and one archer shot two arrows from each of the eighteen tees.

In 1954 at the Southbroom Club, South Africa, a match over nine holes was played between an archer and a fisherman against two golfers. The participants were all champions in their own spheres and consisted of Vernon Adams (archer), Dennis Burd (fisherman), Miss Jeanette Wahl (champion of Southbroom and Port Shepstone), and Ron Burd (professional at Southbroom). The conditions: the archer had holed out when his arrows struck a small leather bag placed on the green beside the hole and, in the event of his placing his approach shot within a bow's length of the pin, he was deemed to have one-putted; the fisherman, to achieve a one-putt, was required to land his sinker within a rod's length of the pin. The two golfers were ahead for brief spells, but it was the opposition that got in front at the deciding ninth hole, where "Robin Hood" played a perfect approach for a birdie.

Freak Matches

In 1912 Harry Dearth, an eminent vocalist, attired in a complete suit of heavy armor, played a match at Bushey Hall. He was beaten by 2 and 1.

In 1914, at the start of the First World War, J. N. Farrar, a native of Hoylake, was stationed at Royston, Herts. A bet was made of ten to one that he would not go round Royston under 100 strokes, equipped in full infantry, marching order, water bottle, full field kit, and haversack. Farrar went round in 94. At

the camp were several golfers, including professionals, who tried the same feat but failed.

Captain Pennington, who was killed in an air crash in 1933, took part in a match "from the air" against A. J. Young, the professional at Sonning. Captain Pennington, with eighty golf balls in the locker of his machine, had to find the Sonning greens by dropping the balls as he circled over the course. The balls were covered in white cloth to ensure that they did not bounce once they struck the ground. The airman completed the course in forty minutes, taking 29 "strokes," while Young occupied two hours for his round of 68.

Milton Reynolds, a United States millionaire, scored an unusual 81 at a golf course in Mexico City by flying from hole to hole in a helicopter.

In April 1924, at Littlehampton, Harry Rowntree, an amateur golfer, played the better ball of Edward Ray and George Duncan, receiving an allowance of 150 yards to use as he required during the round. Rowntree won by 6 and 5 and had used only 50 yards 2 feet of his handicap. At one hole, where Duncan had a 2—Rowntree, who was 25 yards from the hole, took this distance from his handicap and won the hole in one. Ray, who died in 1945, afterward declared that, conceded a handicap of 1 yard per round, he could win every championship in the world. And he might, when reckoning is taken of the number of times a putt just stops an inch or two short or how much difference to a shot three inches will make for the lie of the ball, either in a bunker or on the fairway. Many single matches on the same system have been played. An 18-handicap player opposed to a scratch player should make a close match with an allowance of 50 yards.

Frank Stewart Smith and D. Scott Chisholm, both of Los Angeles, played in a regular monthly tournament of the Southern California Golf Writers' Association in February 1932, with a single club between them. They used a mid-iron, Smith playing right-handed and Chisholm left-handed, and both finished in the low 80's. The club was adapted for either right- or left-handed play.

John Montague, Los Angeles, who gained considerable notoriety in 1937 for his reputed golfing feats, played one hole against a film star, equipped only with a rake and shovel. Montague used the shovel to delve himself out of a bunker, and the head of the rake to hit the ball. The match is mentioned here because of widespread publicity that Montague had played a full round with pick and shovel, but the match was only of one hole.

The first known instance of a golf match by telephone occurred in 1957, when the Cotswold Hills Golf Club, Cheltenham, England, won a golf tournament against the Cheltenham Golf Club, Melbourne, Australia, by six strokes. A large crowd assembled at the English club to wait for the 12,000 mile telephone call from Australia. The match had been played at the suggestion of a former member of the Cotswold Hills Club, Mr. Harry Davies, and was open to every member of the two clubs. The result of the match was decided on the aggregate of the eight best scores on each side, and the English club won by 564 strokes to 570.

Blind and Blindfolded Golf

Major Towse, V.C., whose eyes were shot out during the South African War, 1899, was the first blind man to play golf. The gallant officer's only stipulations when playing were that he should be allowed to touch the ball with his hands to ascertain its position, and that his caddie rang a small bell to indicate the position of the hole. Major Towse, who played with considerable skill, was also an expert oarsman and bridge player. He died in 1945, age eighty-one.

The United States Blind Golfers' Association in 1946 promoted an Invitational Golf Tournament for the blind at Country Club, Inglewood, California. This competition is held annually. In 1953 there were twenty-four competitors, and eleven players completed the two rounds of thirty-six holes. The winner was Charley Boswell, who lost his eyesight leading a tank unit in Germany in 1944.

In July 1954 at Lambton Golf and Country Club, Toronto, the first international championship for the blind was held. It resulted in a win for Joe Lazaro of Waltham, Massachusetts, with a score of 220 for the two rounds. He drove the 215-yard sixteenth hole and just missed an ace, his ball stopping 18 inches from the hole. Charley Boswell was second.

Alfred Toogood played in a match at Sunningdale in 1912

blindfolded. His opponent was Mr. Tindal Atkinson, and Toogood was beaten by 8 and 7. Mr. I. Millar, Newcastle-on-Tyne, played a match, blindfolded, against Mr. A. T. Broughton, Birkdale, at Newcastle, County Down, in 1908. Putting matches while blindfolded have been played frequently.

Wing-Commander "Laddie" Lucas, D.S.O., D.F.C., M.P., played over Sandy Lodge golf course in Hertfordshire on 7 August 1954, completely blindfolded and had a score of 87, which is only 15 above par.

Prize Money, Largest

The world's richest tournament to date is the Dow Jones Open played in August, 1970, at Edison, New Jersey, where the prize money totaled $300,000 ($60,000 top prize money).

The biggest first prize previously awarded was the $55,000 won by Gay Brewer in the Alcan Golfer of the Year Championship inaugurated at St. Andrews in 1967.

The Machrie Tournament of 1901 had a first prize of £100, and was open to both amateurs and professionals. The prize was won by J. H. Taylor, then Open Champion. Braid was his opponent in the final. This was the first £100 prize offered.

Highest Stakes and Large Club Pools

In the seventy-two-hole match between Walter Hagen and Abe Mitchell, played on 18 and 19 June 1926 over Wentworth and St. George's Hill, the stake was £1,000 (£500 a side). Hagen, who was 4 down at the end of the Wentworth section of the match, won by 2 and 1.

A. D. Locke and Sid Brews, South Africa, challenged Reginald Whitcombe, the British Open Champion, and Henry Cotton, for £500 a side, total stake £1,000 in a seventy-two-hole four-ball match. The contest took place in July 1938 at Walton Heath. At the end of thirty-six holes the South Africans were two up. At the end of fifty-four holes the Englishmen were two up, and at the finish they won by 2 and 1. Ten thousand spectators watched the last round.

Hagen, after winning his first British Open Championship, played Gene Sarazen (U.S. Open Champion) at Brooklawn and Biltmore, October 1922. The stake was $3,000, 60 percent to the winner and 40 percent to the loser. Sarazen won by 4 and 3.

In the match between Mr. Bobby Jones and Walter Hagen in 1926, the professional was paid $8,600 from the gate money, the largest sum then won in a single match. Bobby Jones received a set of diamond cuff links.

Large stakes have been played for by amateurs, notably in the match in 1868 when Lord Kennedy played Mr. Cruickshanks, of Langley Park, three holes at St. Andrews for £500 a hole. There can be no accurate record of private wagers, but high stakes are frequently played for by members of several leading golf clubs.

High Scores

Playing in qualifying rounds of the 1965 British Open Championship at Southport, an American self-styled professional entrant from Milwaukee, Walter Danecki, achieved the inglorious feat of scoring a total of 221 strokes for 36 holes, or 83 strokes behind the leader of the qualifiers, or 81 over par. His first round over the Hillside Course was 108. He broke that "Open" record with a second round of 113, made up thus: Out—7-7-8-5-5-7-9-5-5 = 58; In—9-6-10-4-6-5-5-4-6 = 55; total 113. Walter, who afterward admitted he felt "a little discouraged and sad," declared that he entered because he was "after the money." Achievement of this ambition appears to have eluded him.

In 1906 when James Robb beat C. C. Lingen in the final of the British Amateur Championship at Hoylake, they halved the sixth hole in the second round in 9, the highest score for a hole in the final of the Amateur Championship. There was a squally wind, and the sixth hole was difficult to play. Lingen was out of bounds in the orchard from his drive, and after dropping another ball he was caught in sand, and afterward, with his fifth shot, he again found sand on the right of the green. Meanwhile, Robb was awkwardly placed from his tee shot, and played out a few yards for a better lie. He was next caught in the bushes, and, playing out to the side, was too strong, and near a hedge, which caught his fifth shot. His sixth was on the edge of the green. Eventually, after they had each missed a short putt, the hole was halved in 9.

In the first British Open Championship at Prestwick in 1860 a competitor took 21, the highest score for one hole ever recorded in this event. The record is preserved in the archives of the Prestwick Golf Club, where the championship was founded.

In 1950 at the British Open Championship at Troon a German amateur, Herman Tissies, took 15 at the short eighth hole—best known as "the postage stamp." His tee shot landed in one of three bunkers guarding the green. Before he reached the green he was in all three bunkers, playing from one to the other and taking five strokes in one. He finally three-putted. He scored 92 for the round, a courageous recovery after his disaster. This is the second highest score for one hole in the Open Championship.

In 1938 in the final two rounds of the British Open Championship, the players who had qualified for the supreme stage had to contend with a hurricane during the greater part of the day. So fierce was the wind that the players had difficulty in keeping their stance during their swing. Scores of 9 for individual holes were numerous; there were many 10s and one player had 14, the equal of the third highest score ever recorded for a single hole in the Open Championship. To illustrate the fury of the gale the player who took 14 had three shots off the tee swept onto the adjoining Prince's Course. He was then playing 7 off the tee (penalty for out-of-bounds stroke and distance); his seventh shot was on the fairway; his eighth in the rough; his ninth in a bunker; two shots to get out of bunker; twelfth on the green; and two putts. Other players stood back from their putts and saw the ball blown into the hole. The International Golf Traders' Exhibition tent, the largest marquee erected in Great Britain for industrial purposes (100 yards long by 20 yards wide), was torn to ribbons by the gale. The players requiring such high scores were the thirty-seven who had got through the qualifying stages, then the qualifying rounds in the championship proper, and were in the last two rounds of championship. Reginald Whitcombe won with 295.

The highest individual scoring ever known in the rounds connected with the British Open Championship occurred at Muirfield, 1935, when a Scottish professional started 7, 10, 5, 10, and took 65 to reach the ninth hole. Another 10 came at the eleventh, and the player decided to retire at the twelve hole. There he was in a bunker, and after playing four shots he had not regained the fairway.

At the Shawnee Club in the qualifying round of a ladies' competition, the number of entrants was exactly the same number as would qualify, but although everybody was bound to succeed, there were special prizes and so the event had to be

decided. One lady hit a tee shot to a short hole and went into a stream just short of the green. As she was bound to qualify if she finished, she resolved to play out the hole. With her husband she put out in a boat and rowed to where her ball was floating. Shot after shot she made in the water without avail. With every shot her husband received a sort of shower bath, but she stuck to her work. Ultimately she landed the ball a mile and a quarter downstream—and then hit it into a wood. She holed out in 166, and the Shawnee Club presented her with a special cup for qualifying.

In the French Open at St. Cloud in 1968, Brian Barnes took 15 for the short eight hole in the second round. After missing putts at which he hurriedly snatched while the ball was moving, he penalized himself further by standing astride the line of a putt. The amazing result was that he actually took twelve strokes while about 3 feet from the hole.

In the 1927 Shawnee Open, Tommy Armour took twenty-three strokes to the seventeenth hole. Armour had won the American Open Championship a week earlier. In an effort to play the hole in a particular way, Armour hooked ball after ball out of bounds and finished with a 21 on the card. There was some doubt about the accuracy of this figure, and on reaching the clubhouse Armour stated that it should be 23. This is the highest score by a professional in a tournament.

Low Scores

Ben Hogan playing on a par-72 course had 261 strokes—27 under par—an average of 65.25 per round.

Lowest score ever recorded by a woman golfer, 62 by Mickey Wright of Dallas, Texas, on the Hogan Park Course (6,286 yards), at Midland, Texas, in November 1964.

The lowest total for a ninety-hole tournament (five rounds) in Britain was made by Flory van Donck, Belgium, when he won the North British-Harrogate Tournament over the Oakdale course in July 1951. His winning total was 337—69, 67, 67, 66, 68. His four-round total was 269. This is the first occasion on which 70 had been broken in five consecutive rounds in a British tournament.

At Worthing, 1952, Tom Haliburton, in a professional tournament, had a first round of 61, the lowest in a British major tournament, followed by a 65, equaling the world-record total of 126 for two consecutive rounds.

Peter Butler equaled the record score in a major British tournament when he went round Sunningdale Old Course in 61 in the second round of the Bowmaker Tournament, which he won.

In the North British-Harrogate Tournament, over the Oakdale course, in July 1951, Peter Thomson, the twenty-one-year-old

Australian professional, who finished second, holed the course in 62 in the third round. His card read: Out—4, 4, 3, 3, 4, 4, 2, 3, 3 = 30; In—4, 3, 4, 4, 4, 2, 4, 4, 3 = 32. Bernard Hunt in the Spalding Tournament at Worthing, August 1953, in his second round achieved the first nine holes in 28 strokes, the lowest nine holes in a British tournament. Hunt's figures: 3, 3, 3, 3, 3, 4 ,4, 3, 2 = 28. In his 63, Daly did the first nine holes in 29—3, 4, 3, 3, 3, 4, 3, 3, 3, which is the second lowest score for nine holes in a British tournament. Eric Green, John Sheridan, and Charles Ward have also done nine holes in 29 in British professional tournaments.

In February 1955, in the Texas Open at San Antonio, Mike Souchak had a score of 257 for seventy-two holes on this course, which has a par of 71. In his first round his score was 60, made up of 33 out and 27 in, the par figures being 36 and 35. This phenomenal score of 60 ties with Ben Hogan's at Portland, Oregon, in 1946 and Toby Lyon's in the 1952 Texas Open.

Max Banbury had a score of 26 for nine holes in a 1952 competition at Woodstock, Ontario.

Ben Hogan, practicing on a 7,006-yard course at Palm Beach, Florida, went round in 61—eleven under par. On the 510-yard fourteenth, his second shot landed 2 feet from the hole. He wrote on his card: "The lowest round I have ever played."

Kel Nagle (Australia) established a tournament record for the British Isles in 1961 when he won the Irish Hospital Tournament at Woodbrook with a 72-hole total of 260.

Deane Beaman equaled the lowest number of putts in one round in the 1968 Costa Mesa Open with 19.

Low Scoring in Championships

The present low-record score for the British Open Championship is 276, established by Arnold Palmer at Troon in 1962.

The first player to score an average of less than 71 strokes a round in the championship was Gene Sarazen in 1932, when he scored 283 at Prince's. This low-winning score stood for eighteen years, being equaled in 1934 by Henry Cotton, in 1935 by Alf Perry, and in 1949 by A. D. Locke and Harry Bradshaw. In 1950 at Troon, Locke established a new low score of 279, which he equaled at St. Andrews in 1957. In 1958 Peter Thomson (Australia) and Dave Thomas both established at Royal Lytham and St. Anne's new low scores of 278, which was equaled in 1960 at St. Andrews by Kel Nagle (Australia). Then in 1962 Palmer scored 276. It is of interest that, in the following year, 1963, at Royal Lytham and St. Anne's, both Bob Charles (New Zealand) and Phil Rodgers (United States) had scores of 277.

The present record low score for a single round in the championship is 65, established by T. H. Cotton, Sandwich, in 1934; E. C. Brown, St. Anne's, 1958; L. Ruiz, Sandwich, 1958; and P. J. Butler, Muirfield, 1966.

The lowest final thirty-six holes of the championship was recorded by J. Nicklaus at St. Andrews in 1964 with rounds of 66 and 68, while the record for the lowest first thirty-six holes was established by T. H. Cotton at Sandwich in 1934 with rounds of 67 and 65 for a total of 132, which also remains the record for two consecutive rounds in the championship.

The best round by an amateur is 66 by F. R. Stranahan at Troon in 1950.

It is noteworthy that the only championship course not included is Carnoustie, where the best rounds in the British Open Championship are 68 by Ben Hogan in 1953 and Billy Casper in 1968.

In the Southern Section Qualifying Competition for the British Open Championship 1926, played at Sunningdale, Mr. Bobby Jones did rounds of 68 and 66. The round of 66 by Jones may be ranked as one of the most perfect rounds ever played in championship golf. It was the perfection of execution with club and ball. He was 33 out and 33 in. He had 33 putts and 33 other shots. He was three under par each way. He failed to reach the green with his second shot at the ninth, where he ran through, and at the short thirteenth, where he was 6 yards short. The achievement in detail, showing the distance, the number of putts, and the score, are truly worthy of record.

Par	Hole	Distance	Score	No. of Putts
5	1	492	4	2
5	2	454	4	2
4	3	292	4	2
3	4	152	3	2
4	5	417	3	1
4	6	418	4	2
4	7	434	4	2
3	8	165	3	2
4	9	270	4	2
36		3094	33	17

Par	Hole	Distance	Score	No. of Putts
5	10	469	4	2
4	11	267	3	1
4	12	443	4	2
3	13	175	3	1
5	14	503	4	2
3	15	229	3	2
4	16	426	4	2
4	17	442	4	2
4	18	415	4	2
36		3369	33	16

The lowest 18-hole score recorded in championships organized by the Professional Golfers' Association of America is 60. This score has been achieved no less than seven times—by Al Brosch at Brackenridge, Texas, in the 1951 Texas Open; by Bill Nary at El Paso, Texas, in the 1952 El Paso Open; by Ted Kroll at Brackenridge, Texas, in the 1954 Texas Open; by Wally Ulrich at Cavalier Country Club, Virginia, in the 1954 Virginia Beach Open; by Tommy Bolt at Hethersfield Country Club, Connecticut, in the 1954 Insurance City Open; by Mike Souchak at Brackenridge, Texas, in the 1955 Texas Open; and by Sam Snead at Glen Lakes Country Club, Dallas, in the 1957 Dallas Open.

Mr. Francis Ouimet, in the first round of the U.S. Amateur Championship on 14 September 1932, against Mr. George Voigt, did the first nine holes in 30. Mr. Ouimet won by 6 and 5. His golf for the nine holes was the best in the history of the U.S. Amateur Championship. Bobby Jones, in the U.S. Championship in 1927, did the first nine holes in 31, which is the next-best achievement in the U.S. Amateur Championship.

In the U.S. Open Championship at Riviera Country Club, Los Angeles, in 1948, Ben Hogan won with 276, which broke by five strokes R. Guldahl's record for the championship which had stood from 1937. This was beaten by Jack Nicklaus with a score of 275 at Baltusrol in 1967.

Percy Alliss's winning score in Italian Open Championship, 1935, at San Remo, was 262. His rounds were 67, 66, 66, 63 = 262. This is the world's record score for four rounds in a national championship.

Jim Ferrier, Manly, won New South Wales championship at Sydney, 1935, with 266. His rounds were 67, 65, 70, 64, and his score was sixteen strokes better than that of the runner-up. When he made this amazing score Ferrier was twenty and an amateur.

In the fourth round of the British Amateur Championship at Hoylake, 1953, J. Harvie Ward, the holder, did the first nine holes against Frank Stranahan in 32. The figures: 4, 3, 4, 3, 4, 4, 3, 4, 3 = 32. Ward was then two up and finally won by one hole. The figures are noteworthy on a great seaside links like Hoylake. One hole was 527 yards and five holes over 400 yards. The total yardage for the nine holes is 3,474 yards.

Flory van Donck, Belgium, won the French Open Championship at St. Cloud, 1957, with a record score of 266. His figures for the four rounds were 66, 67, 67, 66.

Michael Bonallack, in beating D. Kelley in the final of the English championship in 1968, did the first round at Ganton in a spectacular 61 with only one putt under 2 feet conceded. He was out in 32 and home in 29. The par of the course is 71.

Feats of Endurance

Although golf is not a game where endurance, in the ordinary sense in which the term is employed in sport, is required, there are several instances of feats on the links which demanded great physical exertion.

Stan Gard, member, North Brighton Golf Club, New South Wales, in 1938 completed fourteen rounds and four holes on his home course. The total of 256 holes is the highest recorded in a normal golf course within twenty-four hours. Gard, who underwent special training to ensure that his legs would stand the strain, started his marathon performance at 12:55 A.M., and finished with the aid of car lights at 9:30 P.M. He played consistent golf, his best being 78 in the tenth round, and his worst 92 in the second round. Gard lost seven balls, four during the second round, and played the last six rounds and four holes with the one ball. Once he had to receive massage for a strained tendon in the left foot, while the soles of his shoes were treated specially to harden the leather.

Bruce Sutherland, on the Craiglockhart Links, Edinburgh, started at 8:15 P.M. on 21 June 1927, and played almost continuously until 7:30 P.M., on 22 June 1927. During the night forecaddies with acetylene lamps lit the way, and lost balls were reduced to a minimum. He completed fourteen rounds. The course is extremely hilly, and a large number of steps made the test exacting, and in the later rounds there was drenching rain. The fourteen rounds represented 252 holes. Mr. Sutherland walked over forty miles in achieving his record. His times were first round (8:15 to 9:30), 1 hr. 15 min.; second round (9:32 to 10:52), 1 hr. 20 min.; third round (10:54 to 12:25), 1 hr. 31 min.; fourth round (12:30 to 2:10), 1 hr. 40 min.; fifth round (2:15 to 3:45), 1 hr. 30 min.; sixth round (3:50 to 5:10), 1 hr. 20 min.; seventh round (5:15 to 6:45), 1 hr. 30 min.; eighth round (6:50 to 8:20), 1 hr. 30 min.; ninth round (8:25 to 10:03), 1 hr. 38 min.; tenth round (10:08 to 11:40), 1 hr. 32 min.; eleventh round (11:45 to 1:25), 1 hr. 40 min.; twelfth round (1:35 to 3:12), 1 hr. 37 min.; thirteenth round (3:20 to 5:20), 2 hr.; fourteenth round (5:30 to 7:30), 2 hr. Mr. Sutherland, who was a physical culture teacher, never recovered from the physical strain and died a few years later.

Commander O. R. Wace, R.N. (Retired) played thirteen rounds on the Westgate-on-Sea and Birchington Golf Course on 22 July 1931 (Midsummer Day), driving off at 4:50 A.M. At 9:40 P.M., he sank a long putt for a bogey-4 to complete his thirteenth round. A 4-handicap golfer, Commander Wace averaged 78 strokes per round of the S.S.S. 69 (5,002 yards) course, sinking all putts, his best round being 74 and his worst 86. In all, he played 1,019 strokes and walked nearly 45 miles.

Twice he stopped for baths, but took no meals, and finished in excellent condition apart from foot blisters. In the last of the

thirteen rounds, he played a match against a fellow clubmember, beating him 3 and 2.

On 27 June 1944, C. A. Macey, professional, Crowborough Beacon, at Folkestone Golf Course, did twelve rounds. Starting at 7 A.M. he finished at 10:50 P.M. The course was nine holes at the time. The feat was unique in that about 11 A.M. the shelling warning was hoisted, and the German long-range guns began a bombardment. It did not last long. Macey played with a set of borrowed clubs. Four different people acted as caddies, including an NCO and a Kent policeman. Macey stopped only once, fifteen minutes, at 1 P.M. His score, 949 shots, averaged 79 for the eighteen holes. Distance walked, approximately 40 miles. Folkestone golf course had over one hundred bomb craters and many shell holes.

Mr. H. T. Peter and Allan Robertson played Mr. O'Brien Peter and old Tom Morris at St. Andrews for two days consecutively, five rounds each day, and the match ended in a draw. When they finished, Allan said wistfully, "I never had sic a bellyfu' o' gowf a' my days."

In 1916 Charles M. Daniels, a champion swimmer, played 228 holes on the Sabatth's Park course in fifteen hours. The green consists of nine holes, measuring 2,174 yards, and in the allotted time Mr. Daniels played 25 nine-hole rounds, with three holes thrown in for luck. His average score was a fraction over 38 strokes per round. He had been training rigorously for the affair, and he started at 4 A.M., had a twenty-minute breakfast at 8 A.M., a quick lunch at noon, and a three-minute rest for a glass of milk at 4 P.M. After that he went on furiously playing golf until 7:30 P.M. At the finish he had covered approximately 35 miles.

In 1923 Dan Kenney, professional at Tyler Country Club, Texas, and William Lundberg, professional at the Glenbrooke Country Club, Houston, Texas, on 7 June 1923, completed 216 holes. The match started at 4:30 A.M., headlights from automobiles being used to light the first fairway and tee. At 8 P.M., when the last hole was completed, it was necessary to use flashlights. Kenney played the 216 holes in 957 strokes, Lundberg 1,003 strokes.

In 1957, Bert L. Scoggins, a United States serviceman, played 260 holes in one day on the American golf course at Berlin. He started out at 2:30 A.M., and played continuously for 18 hours, walking 56 miles in the course of his marathon feat. His lowest single round score was 84.

Bill Falkingham, Jr., of Amstel Golf Club, Victoria, Australia, played 257 holes between 12:30 A.M. and 6:15 P.M. on 14 December 1968, the first three holes having been played in darkness. He was accompanied by his brother and a friend who held a torch to assist direction. Ten balls were lost, but the first ball lasted eight rounds. His best round was 90 over a course measuring 6,673 yards, par-73, over which a gale force wind blew all day, in a temperature of 90 degrees. During the morning he trod on a snake but did not stop to kill it. He was sustained by only sandwiches and soft drinks and, although completely exhausted when he finished, he had recovered next morning and went out for another round.

A world record is claimed by Ed Lincoln, Harrisburg, who completed 270 holes between 5:10 A.M. and 6:30 P.M., Overlook Country Club, Pennsylvania, during 1969. He rode over the course, however, and had his ball teed up by helpers who also acted as spotters. His highest round was 92 and his lowest 70. The course measured 6,052 yards.

Bill Fleenor, seventeen years of age, of Walla Walla Country Club, Washington, having heard of Ed Lincoln's feat, started out at 5 A.M. at Walla Walla and by 5:45 P.M. had completed 275 holes, his highest score being 88 and lowest 78. It is not reported whether he had any assistance in this remarkable effort.

Freak Endurance Tests and Many Courses Played Within Twenty-four Hours

Four Aberdeen University students, as a 1961 Charities Week stunt, set out to golf their way up Ben Nevis (4,406 feet). After losing 63 balls and expending 659 strokes, the quartet, about halfway up, conceded victory to Britain's highest mountain.

Endurance feats serve no purpose, and ridiculous forms of marathon golf have been perpetrated in United States. The following "feats" which were given worldwide press publicity at the time they were said to have been accomplished are recorded merely as freaks and verging on the impossible even for small golf courses or what in America are designated Tom Thumb courses, and as illustrating the varied forms of stupidity which can be displayed in manufacturing stunts for exploitation and securing personal vainglorious publicity in the press.

An American claimed to have played in 1931 at Purchase Country Club, New York, 246 holes, during which he asserted he walked 70 miles. The time occupied was 21 hours 15 minutes. The distance compared to the time makes this claim preposterous. In the same year Sir Oliver Lambert, an Irish baronet, age eighteen, was reported to have played 254 holes. His only food was reported to have been a sandwich, a glass of lemonade, and two glasses of milk.

An amazing "endurance achievement" was carried through by Edward A. Ferguson of the American School of Theatre Arts at Detroit, Michigan, on the nine-hole Ridgemont Golf Course of that city. The course is a small public one. Ferguson started out at 6 P.M. on 25 August 1930 to play golf continuously for twenty-four hours. After completing his first twenty-four hours Ferguson decided to go right on, and at the end of a week he claimed to have walked 327½ miles and played 92 times round the nine-hole course in 3,999 strokes. Ferguson mapped out a scheme of resting. The test cannot be compared with the endurance feats accomplished on full-size golf courses, but this astonishing performance is worthy of reference here. In the off-season, actors have many peculiar hobbies. Ferguson had played little golf prior to his "endurance feat." He wrote for *The Golfer's Handbook* his own story of how he came to attempt the feat and what happened.

My wife and I were talking one night about all the different marathons that had been going on, everything from Cross-Country runs to Dancing and Tree Sitting. My wife said, "The only thing that they have missed is Golf." That gave me the idea, so I started out to play for twenty-four hours.

I started out on the first nine at 6 P.M., 25 August 1930. I was to have ten minutes' rest between each nine holes, but with the crowd of people wanting autographed golf balls and pictures, and telephone calls to and from newspapers, I finally gave up the idea of resting, and would play straight through, thus piling up time to eat. I had about three hours and a half coming to me when I quit.

I got one "Hole in one" on the 11th the first night; later an Eagle, and my "Ringer Score" (the best of each of the 18 holes of the 92 rounds) was 55. The Par is 72.

The night play was accomplished with the aid of a barn lantern and a pocket flashlight, in the hand of the caddie, who would stand on the green on short holes and midway between tee and green on the long holes. The ball was painted with luminous paint, making it easier to find on the ground. The "gallery" ran from about 25 in the wee small hours to mobs of I cannot say how many in the daytime and at night. In the early morning hours I would have a lot of golf pros and newspaper men in the "gallery"—waiting to see me go to sleep, but they were disappointed.

I suffered no ill effects from the play whatsoever, but I did gain five pounds in weight during that week. I walked 327½ miles from tee to green, not counting hooks and slices. I quit on 1 September at 8 o'clock in the morning. My hands were covered with soft callouses and blisters, and I could not control the club. I had played 158 hours, with an average slightly over 86 for each 18 holes.

Colonel B. Farnham played 376 holes of the Guilford Lake Course, Guilford, Connecticut, in 24 hours 10 minutes, using only a mashie and a putter. A short course and a race rather than golf, as the average time per round was less than 1 hour 10 minutes.

Robert Coy, at Peoria, Illinois, claimed that in 51½ hours he played 1,000 successive holes. He asserted he employed 25 caddies and during the night he had the aid of lights. The character of the "feat" and the course may best be judged by the fact that 1,000 holes represents 60 rounds, so that Coy on each round occupied 51 minutes, without allowing for stoppages.

In October 1938, J. Smith Ferebee, a Chicago broker, played 600 holes of golf in a tour across the United States in four days. Ferebee used an airplane to fly between the cities in which he played. On the first day he played 84 holes at Los Angeles and 81 at Phoenix, Arizona; on the second, 72 at Kansas City and 72 at St. Louis; on the third, 72 at Milwaukee and 75 at Chicago; and on the fourth, 72 at Philadelphia and 72 at New York. To crown the absurdity of this "golf marathon" it was reported in newspapers throughout the world that Ferebee and his backers won $150,000 in wagering and the sole rights in a $30,000 plantation.

In Ferebee's press stunt it was claimed he had set the seal on golf marathons.

Sidney Gleave, motorcycle racer, and Ernest Smith, golf professional, Davyhulme Club, Manchester, on 12 June 1939, played five rounds of golf in five different countries—Scotland, Ireland, Isle of Man, England, and Wales. Smith had to play the five rounds under 80 in one day to win the £100 wager. They flew, and the following was their schedule with time taken and Smith's score:

Start—Prestwick St. Ninian (Scotland), 3:40 A.M. Score 70. Time taken, 1 hour 35 minutes.

Second course—Bangor (Ireland), 7:15 A.M. Score 76. Time taken, 1 hour 30 minutes.

Third course—Castletown (Isle of Man), 10:15 A.M. Score 76. Time taken, 1 hour 40 minutes.

Fourth course—Blackpool, Stanley Park (England), 1:30 P.M. Score 72. Time taken, 1 hour 55 minutes.

Fifth course—Hawarden (Wales), 6 P.M. Score 68 (record). Time, 2 hours 15 minutes.

Guy Price, nineteen-year-old Southern Californian, in 1939, played eighteen rounds in sixteen different states, teeing up in Los Angeles for his first round and holing out at Fresh Meadow, New York, for his eighteenth round. He traveled by car 12,340 miles, including the detours, from coast to coast and back again, to reach the various golf courses.

Grant Bennett, twenty-nine-year-old professional at North Carolina, Golf Club, August 1949, completed th. rounds, plus one hole, a total of 343 holes in twenty-four . The course measures 3,075 yards. The feat was elaborately or. ized. Between shots, Bennett was conveyed by an auto. Durin. the night a squad of caddies marked the ball, and along the line of play were stationed aides who pulled out the club and replaced it in the bag after Bennett hit the shot. Bennett took 1,477 shots, an average of 38.71 strokes per round of nine holes. He played the first three rounds in a rainstorm and finished in a rainstorm. His hands were badly blistered and in the later rounds were bleeding badly. The feat, extraordinary as an endurance test, cannot be compared with those who engaged in record marathons, because Bennett was conveyed from shot to shot and had assistance handling his clubs.

Since the conclusion of war in 1945 few purposeless freaks have been perpetrated. One occurred in 1953 when J. Smith, an American amateur, for an amazing wager of $25,000 won the bet to play 600 holes of golf in eight cities in four days and to break 90 in each round. He flew over 3,000 miles, actually walked 180 miles on the eight courses. He employed 110 caddies, having four when he played at night to guide him in the darkness with torches and flares. The only rest he had in the four days was when traveling by airplane. The holes he played: Los Angeles, 84 holes; Phoenix, Arizona, 81; Kansas City, 72; St. Louis, 72; Milwaukee, 75; Chicago, 72; Philadelphia, 72; New York City, 72. He played 36 holes in Phoenix, Arizona, after 9 P.M. and broke 80 in each round. A ridiculously crazy but wonderful feat of endurance.

Record Drives

A sloping ground, especially if frost-bound, and a following wind, will assist a ball immensely on its course, and exceptional distances have been driven on links hardened like cement by frost or parched dry in midsummer.

The United States PGA record drive is 341 yards, recorded by Jack Nicklaus in July 1963.

The long-driving competition, held at the British Open Championships in 1922, 1923, 1924, 1925, and 1926, contributed reliable data to distances achieved in driving. In this series of five competitions engaged in by the longest drivers known at the time, hitting all out and under favorable conditions, the longest individual drive was 290 yards 10 inches, thus proving that any drive approaching 300 yards must be attended by abnormal and favorable circumstances to aid its distance after its first contact with the ground.

In the first competition at Sandwich the conditions were what could be properly described as normal: the ground was fairly level with run at the end, if anything, against the ball; wind, cross, but slightly with the direction of flight; and the fairway dry, very much as it is found on any average June month. A. Easterbrook (Sidmouth) had the longest individual drive, 277 yards 9½ inches. John Smith (Cantelupe Club, Forest Row) won the competition with an aggregate of 532 yards 8½ inches for his two best drives.

The long-driving competition at Troon in 1923 was competed for by every notable professional, and the data largely confirmed the distances of the previous year.

At the championship, June 1924, the contest took place on the Hoylake ladies' course. There was a very slight and scarcely perceptible wind against the drivers. J. Smith, who won the first year and was not a competitor at Troon, won the cup with a total of 728 yards for three drives, or an average of 242 yards 8 inches.

In 1925 the competition was held at Troon, Portland, on the identical ground as in 1923. The best three out of five drives counted. The conditions were normal, wind slightly favoring. The cup was won by J. W. Milner, with a total for three drives of 842 yards 1 foot 9 inches, or an average of 280 yards 2 feet 7 inches.

In 1926, at St. Anne's, Archie Compston won the competition for the longest drive and also the competition for the best average of three out of four balls. Compston's longest drive was 288 yards 3 inches, and his average 263 yards 6½ inches.

In 1938 a series of official tests were carried out on British courses. At Moortown, during the English Amateur Championship, the average flight of the ball (without run) was 214.38 yards. During the Walker Cup match at St. Andrews in May, the average was 218.8 yards—identical with the figures provided by tests at Troon during the Amateur Championship. At Malone (Ireland), in May, with the wind against the players, the average was 210 yards. Those official tests were made to provide data for considering the question of reducing the length of flight of the golf ball.

At the international match, Portmarnock, 1949, a driving competition was held in which all the players from the four nations—England, Scotland, Ireland and Wales—competed. The actual carry was measured. The Irishmen proved the longest drivers. The best distances of carry:

Ireland.	J. Bruen	280
	J. B. Carr	265
	J. Carroll	250
	W. M. O'Sullivan	250
	J. Burke	235
	S. M. McCready	235
	B. J. Scannell	235
England.	G. H. Micklem	235
	P. B. Lucas	235
	K. Thom	235
	D. Rawlinson	235
Scotland.	J. B. Stevenson	235
	A. S. Flockhart	235
Wales.	A. D. Evans	230
	M. Jones	230

From an analytical point of view, one might be justified in saying that the long-driving competitions supplied precise information that very long hitters, when they are all out for length, can succeed in hitting a golf ball about 270 yards, but that the average length of their tee shots is probably between 230 and 240 yards, and the man who can maintain an average of over 230 yards must be considered to be an exceedingly good wooden-club player. At the various long-driving competitions the players were positively swiping every ounce that was in them, and many shots went out of bounds.

On 10 August 1937 at Fonthill, Ontario, a long-driving competition was held, and James Thomson, the Scottish-American professional, reckoned the longest driver in the United States, won the prize of $1,000 with a drive of 286 yards ½ inch. Thomson's winning shot, therefore, made eleven years after the last driving competition at the Open Championship, confirms the opinion expressed in the foregoing paragraph.

In the final round of the 1970 British Open Championship, at the 358-yard eighteenth, Jack Nicklaus hit his drive through the back of the green, an estimated 380 yards, on the Old Course, St. Andrews.

The late Douglas Rolland was undoubtedly the biggest hitter among professional golfers in the era of the gutta ball. By the time the rubber ball came into use, Rolland was an invalid. At the Open Championship at Sandwich in 1894, Rolland was at the zenith of his form and manhood and was driving a prodigious distance. At that meeting there was a match between amateurs and professionals, and Rolland played against Mr. John Ball. Their respective drives were marked and afterward measured, and it was found that Rolland's longest tee shot was 235 yards and that his average for the round was 205 yards for each drive he played at holes where length was a consideration, and that Mr. Ball's average was 198 yards. This represented mighty fine hitting with a solid ball and may be taken as a fair indication of the very longest distances possible with a gutta ball under normal conditions.

The following drives are recorded here as interesting events, but it must not be lost sight of that in every case conditions were more or less abnormal, either frozen ground, or the ground hard through drought, or a fierce following wind, or considerable fall from tee to hole, or a combination of these various favoring elements, and the drives are given as curiosities.

E. C. Bliss at Herne Bay, August 1913, hit a distance of 445 yards. The drive was measured, and levels taken by Mr. L. H. Lloyd, government surveyor, who measured the drop in the ground from the tee to the resting place, and the fall was 57 feet.

Craig Wood, in playing off the tie in the British Open Championship with Denny Shute at St. Andrews, June 1933, had an amazing drive at the fifth hole. The hole, the longest at St. Andrews, was stretched to its limit. The length was 530 yards. Wood drove into the bunker in the face of the hill short of the green. From the position of the hole on the green, at the time, to the edge of the bunker was 97 yards; and allowing for 3 yards in the bunker—it is a wide bunker—the ball was approximately 100 yards short of the hole, making Craig Wood's drive 430 yards.

114

There was a considerable following wind, the day bright and sunny, and the ground parched following prolonged dry, hot weather.

At Sitwell Park, Rotherham (Yorkshire), 1935, W. Smithson, the home professional, drove the second green from the competition tee, the hole measuring 416 yards. There was a following wind, but Smithson's feat is remarkable for the fact that he carried over a dike which runs across the hole at a distance of 380 yards from the tee. The remaining distance is a steep uphill approach to the green, and his ball finished pin high.

W. E. Macnamara, professional at Lahinch, County Clare, in 1913, playing with Mr. F. S. Bond, Royal Wimbledon, drove to the fourth green at Lahinch, a distance of 400 yards. About 250 yards from the tee, and, running right across the center of the course, was a huge sand bunker about 25 feet high, called the Klondyke. To get into that bunker from the tee was one of the very best shots. Macnamara, in describing his drive states, "How the ball ever got where it was I do not know unless that it happened to bounce on a stone or something very hard at the end of 250 yards and then run the rest of the distance down the hill. I believe that if all the best players in the world were to drive at that tee all their lives, I do not think the same thing would happen again." Macnamara's drive is specially notable, not alone for its length but because it carried a bunker at 250 yards from the tee.

On 13 October 1929, at Royal Wimbledon Golf Club's course,

Mr. T. H. V. Haydon, a member of the club, drove a ball to the fifteenth hole, a distance of 420 yards. The ball finished just short of the green on an upslope. The fairway is slightly uphill all the way. It was a bright, warm day with a following breeze with the ground dry as it had not rained for several days. This feat was confirmed by Mr. H. C. C. Tippett, the secretary of the Royal Wimbledon Golf Club.

Long Carries

Using a No. 2 wood, George Bell, a member of the Penrith Club, New South Wales, Australia, drove a golf ball across the Nepean River, a certified carry of 309 yards. He drove off a coir mat on the back of a truck in the annual "King of the River" driving contest, 1964.

Playing in the £500 Challenge Match at Walton Heath on 27 July 1938, partnered by Reg Whitcombe against Bobbie Locke and Sid Brews, Henry Cotton drove across the corner of the doglegged twelfth and reached the green. The hole, played in the normal manner, is 370 yards, but the straight line which Cotton took is 280 yards with a vast expanse of bushes and ferns to carry to a small patch of grass before the green. He chipped up and got a birdie-3 to win the hole.

Great Golf Matches

It would be impossible to give a detailed list here of great matches decided about the time when Allan Robertson, the Morrises, the Dunns, and the Parks were in their zenith, but the following are a few of the biggest matches that were played in an interesting period of golfing history and subsequently:

1843: Allan Robertson, St. Andrews, beat Willie Dunn, Musselburgh, in a match of 20 rounds, 300 holes, by 2 rounds and 1 to play.

1849: Allan Robertson and Tom Morris, of St. Andrews, beat the brothers Dunn, of Musselburgh, over Musselburgh, St. Andrews, and North Berwick, for a stake of £400. The Dunns won at Musselburgh by 13 up and 12; but Robertson and Morris got even at St. Andrews. The match, therefore, reverted to North Berwick. The Dunns were 4 up and 8 to play. Odds of 20 to 1 were laid on the Dunns at this point; but Robertson and Morris won by 1 hole.

1853: Willie Park, Sr., twice defeated Tom Morris, Sr., in £100 matches. Allan Robertson was repeatedly challenged by Park, but refused to play.

1854–55: Park and Morris played in all six £100 matches, and honors were about evenly divided. In the fifth match at Musselburgh the spectators interferred with Morris's ball repeatedly, and the referee stopped play. Morris and the referee, Bob Chambers, an Edinburgh publisher, retired to a nearby public house. Park waited for some time and then sent a message to Chambers and Morris that if they did not come out to play to a finish he himself would play the remaining holes and claim the stakes. Morris and Chambers remained in the public house, and Park, completing the round, was subsequently awarded the stakes.

1868: Lord Kennedy and Mr. Cruikshank, of Langley Park, played a match of three holes for £500 a hole at St. Andrews. Play started at 10 P.M., and the only light was given by lamps stuck on the flagpins of the three holes. It is not known who won this extraordinary match.

1875: Old and Young Tom Morris beat Willie Park and Mungo Park for £50 at North Berwick by one hole. This was the last big money match Young Tom played. A telegram had been received in North Berwick before the end of the match intimating that Young Tom's wife had died. The news was kept from him until he boarded John Lewis's yacht, which took the St. Andrews party across the Forth. Young Tom never recovered from the news, and he died on Christmas Day of the same year, age twenty-five.

1896: Willie Park defeated J. H. Taylor in a seventy-two-hole match over Musselburgh and Sudbrook Park. The match was notable for the rowdyism of the spectators at Musselburgh, and there was so much local partisanship that three years later Harry Vardon definitely refused to include Musselburgh as Park's home course in their great match, and Park had to take North Berwick.

1899: Harry Vardon, in a seventy-two-hole match (36 holes over North Berwick and 36 holes over Ganton), defeated Willie Park, Jr., by 11 and 10 for £100 a side. At the end of thirty-six holes at North Berwick, Vardon was two holes up. The first ten holes were halved. At the eleventh hole, Park had the honor and Vardon's drive pitched on Park's ball and rebounded 2 feet. Vardon duffed his next shot and lost the hole—the first change in the match. The spectators at North Berwick numbered over 10,000, and represented an unprecedented attendance for an individual match up to that time and for many years afterward.

1904: The brothers Harry and Tom Vardon defeated James Braid and Jack White at Sunningdale in a thirty-six-hole match by 3 and 1. They also won the last hole.

1905: J. H. Taylor and Harry Vardon, representing England, defeated James Braid and Alex Herd, representing Scotland, by 13 and 12 over four greens, for £200 a side. Green results: St. Andrews—Scotland, 2 up; Troon—England, 12 up; St. Anne's—England, 7 up; Deal—England won by 13 up and 12. At Troon the attendance equaled the great crowd at North Berwick for the Vardon-Park match.

1908: George Duncan and Charles Mayo beat Tom Vardon and Edward Ray in a seventy-two-hole match for £200 over Deal and Princes by 6 and 5.

1910: Miss C. Leitch (Silloth), receiving a half handicap, beat Mr. H. H. Hilton in a seventy-two-hole match over Walton Heath and Sunningdale by 2 and 1. At the end of the Walton Heath leg Mr. Hilton was 2 up.

1922: Gene Sarazen beat Walter Hagen in a seventy-two-hole match over Brooklawn and Westchester Country Club, Biltmore, by 3 and 2. Hagen was 2 up at end of thirty-six holes. Stake, $3,000.

1926: Walter Hagen beat Mr. Bobby Jones in a seventy-two-hole match at St. Petersburg and Sarasota Bay by 11 and 10. Hagen was paid $5,000 for the St. Petersburg half and received all the gate money at $3 per ticket at Sarasota. The gate money was $3,500. Hagen's combined fee of $8,500 was the largest ever received by a professional golfer for a challenge match. Hagen presented Mr. Jones with a set of shirt studs and cuff links.

1927: Harry Cooper beat George Duncan in a seventy-two-hole match at Los Angeles by 7 and 5. At end of thirty-six holes Cooper was 4 up. The match was currently reported in the press as one for a stake of £1,000, but the players were paid $250 each for their services, and there was no private or side stake of the magnitude reported.

1928: Archie Compston, on April 27 and 28, at Moor Park, London, defeated Walter Hagen in a seventy-two-hole match by 18 and 17. At the end of the thirty-six holes, Compston was fourteen holes up. This is the greatest margin of victory ever recorded in a first-class professional match. Stake, £500. Hagen proceeded to Sandwich, where he won for the third time the Open Championship.

1937: Henry Cotton, Open Champion, beat Densmore Shute, American professional champion, over seventy-two holes at Walton Heath. At the end of eighteen holes they were all square, at thirty-six holes Cotton was two up, at fifty-four holes (end third round) Cotton was 5 up, and he won by 6 and 5. The match followed immediately after the Open Championship at Carnoustie. A sum of £500 was put up to be won outright, but the donor, when the winning check was handed to Cotton, also presented Shute with £100.

The Fastest Rounds

At Mowbray Course, Cape Town, November 1931, Len Richardson, who had represented South Africa in the Olympic games, played a round which measured 6,248 yards in 31 minutes 22 seconds.

Dr. E. W. Joscelyne, Radyr, played the eighteen holes of this course in June 1909 in 44 minutes. The wager was that he could not hole out every hole and finish in 45 minutes. Dr. Joscelyne was attired in running costume, and used a cleek only to play with.

In 1928, Levett, an athlete, training for a run from Los Angeles to New York, as part of his preparation raced round Palos Verdes Golf Links hitting a golf ball. He was attired in running costume, and his best time for the course was 43 minutes. The course was 6,107 yards. He holed out at each hole.

On 14 June 1922, Jock Hutchison and Joe Kirkwood (Australia) played round the Old Course at St. Andrews in 1 hour 20 minutes. Hutchison, out in 37, led by three holes at the ninth and won by 4 and 3.

K. Bousfield and J. Knipe, two assistants, completed six rounds of golf in 3 minutes over 12 hours on Burnham Beeches, 20 September 1938. They set out at 7 A.M. and despite rain maintained good progress—until the last round, when they had to run to do the final eighteen holes in 1 hour 28 minutes. The haste did not upset Bousfield, for he completed the final round in 69—one over the course record. Bousfield took 437 strokes for the six rounds and Knipe 449.

In 1939, at Tam O'Shanter Club, Niles, Illinois, an army of players took part in a round to ascertain how quickly a ball could be propelled round the course, which was 6,400 yards long. The players stood at selected points to hit the ball from the tee, the fairway, and to putt, and a caddie stood at each hole to pitch the ball, the moment it was holed out, onto the next tee. There were spare players near the bunkers which were likely to be visited, so that the ball could be propelled on without loss of time. It took 17 minutes 20 seconds, just under 1 minute per hole, for the ball to go right round the course.

A relay team of twenty-five Cape Town University students in 1964 played the eighteen holes of the Rodebosch Course (6,120 yards) in 13 minutes 53.4 seconds.

At Walla Walla Country Club, in 1950, a relay team of twenty players holed nine holes in 7 minutes 3 seconds. The team took 41 strokes.

At Sim Park Golf Club, Kansas, in 1950, a team of thirty-four players played a ball round nine holes in 5 minutes 23 seconds.

At Monroe Golf Club, Michigan, in 1951, fifty-three players were placed at different points round the course. They holed nine holes in 5 minutes 14 seconds, taking 44 strokes.

Oldest and Youngest Champions

Roberto de Vicenzo was forty-four when he won the British Open Championship in 1967; Ted Ray forty-three when he won the U.S. Open in 1920; Sam Snead forty-one when he won the U.S. Masters Tournament in 1954, and 52 years, 10 months and 7 days when he won the 1965 Greensboro Open, becoming the oldest winner of a USPGA tournament; and Julius Boros forty-eight when he won the USPGA Championship in 1968. These are the oldest winners of these four major events.

Jack Westland (Seattle) won the U.S. Amateur Championship, 1952, at the age of forty-seven, the oldest player to win this championship. Twenty-one years before (1931), Westland was defeated in the final by Francis Ouimet, 6 and 5.

Harry Vardon, when he won his sixth British Open Championship in 1914, was fifty-one days younger than Roberto de Vicenzo in 1967.

Tom Morris, Jr., won the first of his four British Open Championships at Prestwick in 1868, when he was eighteen years of age. This record has never been surpassed.

The Honorable Michael Scott, at Hoylake in 1933, won the British Amateur Championship at the age of fifty-four, the oldest player to become the Champion Amateur Golfer. Mr. Charles Hutchings won the British Amateur Championship, also at Hoylake, in 1902, at the age of fifty-three. His first grandchild was born the same day.

The most pronounced instance of precocity in the history of the game in Great Britain stands to the credit of Mr. John Ball, who, at the age of fifteen, finished sixth in the British Open Championship at Prestwick in 1878. His score for the thirty-six holes, of which the competition then consisted, was 165, and he was eight strokes behind the winner, Jamie Anderson.

Mr. Bobby Jones at the age of seventeen won the Southern Amateur Championship in the United States.

The youngest player ever to win the United States Open was John J. McDermott, Jr., who, at the age of nineteen years, ten months, and fourteen days won a play-off with Mike Brady and George Simpson at Wheaton, Illinois, on 26 June 1911. McDermott retained his title by winning the Open again in 1912, at Buffalo, New York.

Mr. Francis Ouimet in 1913 won the U.S. Open Championship in his twentieth year after a tie with Harry Vardon and Ted Ray.

In his twentieth year, Mr. A. G. Barry won the British Amateur Championship at Prestwick in 1905.

When fifteen years of age, Mr. Fred Ballingall, Blairgowrie, won the South of Ireland Championship from a strong field, defeating in the final Mr. John Gairdner, a Scottish international player. In his eighteenth year Mr. Ballingall won the cup outright by virtue of three victories.

When fifteen years of age, Lord Charles Hope won the sweepstakes in the St. George's Cup, at Sandwich, from a handicap of 6.

Young Tom Morris, born in 1850, won the British Open Championship in 1868. In his twentieth year he won the championship belt outright, and when twenty-two he won the Open Championship for the fourth time. Had the championship not lapsed for one year after Young Tom's winning the belt, this great golfing genius might have added to his achievement, which still stands as a record, of four successive championship victories. Young Tom at the age of sixteen won an open professional tournament at Montrose. He died at the age of twenty-five.

Willie Park, at the age of fourteen, left Musselburgh and became an assistant professional to his uncle Mungo Park, at Alnmouth. When fifteen years of age Park was appointed professional to Ryton-on-Tyne and occupied the position for some years.

When seventeen years of age, Miss May Hezlet won the Irish Ladies' Championship and the Ladies' Championship in successive weeks at Newcastle, County Down, in 1899.

Miss Pamela Barton, Royal Mid-Surrey, in 1934, won the French Ladies' Championship at the age of seventeen and in 1936 won the British Ladies' Championship at Southport and the American Ladies' Championship at Canoe Brook, New Jersey, when nineteen years of age. This brilliant and lovable golfer was killed serving in the WAAF in the Second World War.

J. D. A. Langley (Boy Champion, 1935) was in his eighteenth year when he played for Great Britain in the 1936 Walker Cup match at Pine Valley, United States. James Bruen (Boy Champion, 1936) was also in his eighteenth year when he played in the top foursomes and top single in the Walker Cup match at St. Andrews, in 1938, when Britain was victorious for the first time. They are the youngest players who have played in this match for the British Isles.

Ladies in Open Competitions and First Lady Club Officials

The entry for the 1962 British Open Championship (at Troon) of Mrs. E. Beck (Wentworth), the first woman professional to enter for this event, was refused by the Royal and Ancient's Championship Committee, on the ground that the inclusion of women competitors had never been contemplated.

Mlle Genevieve le Derff, woman professional at Fourqueux

and Paris, competed in the French Open Championship at Four-queux on 24 September 1929. This was the first occasion a woman had competed in a national open championship.

Miss Poppy Wingate, when assistant at Templenewsam Course, Leeds, competed in the Leeds Professional Tournament in May 1933. This was the first time a woman competed in a British professional tournament. Miss Meg Farquhar, who had been an assistant professional at Moray Golf Club and was an assistant in a golf clubmaker's shop in Elgin, on 7–8 June 1933 competed in the Scottish professional championship at Lossie-mouth. She was twenty-two, and her total of 333 for the four rounds was 30 strokes better than some of her male rivals. She was the first woman to compete in a professional championship in Scotland. These two women competed again in open professional events.

Helen Hicks, the former U.S. Amateur Champion who turned professional in 1935, was touring Australia with Gene Sarazen when in September 1936, at Melbourne, she competed in the South Australia Open Championship. She was the first woman to compete in a professional championship in Australia.

In the Cruden Bay Tournament, 3 July 1919, Mrs. Alan Mac-Beth (Miss Muriel Dodd, winner of the Ladies' Championship, 1913) competed. This was the first occasion a lady competed in an open tournament.

Miss Ida Kyle and Miss Mollie Griffiths competed in the Eden Tournament at St. Andrews in 1921. Neither succeeded in qualifying for the match-play stage. After this year it was not unusual for ladies to play in open-stroke tournaments.

In May 1927, a team of ladies competed in the Braid Hills (Edinburgh) Tournament. The competition is decided by foursomes, and the ladies were Mrs. J. B. Watson, Scottish Ladies Champion, 1920-21-22; Miss Mary Wood, Scottish Ladies Champion, 1926; Miss Doris Park (Mrs. Aylmer Porter), Scottish Lady Champion, 1937; and Miss Edith Nimmo. The ladies were beaten in the first round. This was the first occasion a team of ladies competed on level terms in an open tournament. In the succeeding year a condition of this competition debarred women entrants.

In 1939, Babe Didrikson (Mrs. Zaharias), Ladies' Champion, 1947, wished to compete in the Australian Open Championship, but her entry was declined. At that time "the Babe" was a professional golfer.

Hole in 0 and Minus 1

A hole for which the score 0 was properly entered on the card was returned in the Middlesex Alliance four-ball medal competition at Northwood, 1934. D. Fraser, Pinner Hill, 6 handicap, holed his tee shot, with an iron, at the fifteenth hole, which measures 150 yards. Fraser received a stroke allowance at the hole, so his net score was 0. At Addington, 1949, J. H. Page Wood holed the eleventh (135 yards) in one. He had a stroke at this hole and properly entered his score as 0.

James Braid was playing at Walton Heath, and his opponent holed in one. Braid was conceding a stroke allowance at the hole. Braid could not even get a half if he had holed in one as his opponent had done the hole in 0, so he picked up his ball and walked to the next tee.

At Cathcart Castle Golf Club, Glasgow, on 23 July 1965, Mr. R. Murdoch had the first hole (173 yards) in one. As he had a handicap stroke at this hole, his score was 0. This was Mr. Murdoch's third "ace," including a par-4 hole at Hayston, near Glasgow.

At Crichel Park, Wimborne, Dorset, 16 April 1939, two brothers, Cooper Vaughan and Edmund Vaughan, did the fourth hole, 178 yards, in one. Cooper Vaughan was conceding his brother a stroke at the hole so that Edmund Vaughan did the hole in 0 on handicap. The incident was certified by the secretary of the Crichel Park Golf Club. The brothers Vaughan started golf in Burma in 1909 and played together regularly, after their retirement for ten years at Crichel Park, before the "miracle" in golf, two brothers holing in one, with one in receipt of a stroke at a particular hole.

On 15 March 1941 over the Digboi Golf Course, Upper Assam, Mr. E. V. Corps did the sixteenth in one and, receiving a stroke at this hole, therefore did it in 0 net. The feat is vouched for by Mr.

A. J. Tyrie, Mr. Corps's opponent, and by Mr. L. F. C. Deane, then honorary secretary of the course.

Mr. A. Henderson, the secretary of Blairgowrie Golf Club, playing over the course on 31 July 1954 in a friendly game with Mr. J. Raymond Scott, holed his tee shot at the eighth hole, a distance of 150 yards. As he was receiving a stroke at this hole he, therefore, did it in 0. This was the second occasion on which Mr. Henderson had holed his tee shot when in receipt of a stroke.

Harry Fulford played a match at Newquay in which he conceded a stroke and a half a hole. His opponent having won a hole had the honor at the next short hole where he had two strokes. He holed his tee stroke, thus doing the hole in minus one.

Mrs. K. N. Corby of the Kenilworth Club holed her tee shot at the 137-yard second hole. As she was receiving two strokes, she scored a net -1

In August 1956, while playing in the Royal and Ancient's Jubilee Vase Competiton at St. Andrews, Michael Gardiner-Hill holed his tee shot at the eighth. As he was receiving a stroke he actually won the hole with a net 0.

At Royal Cinque Ports Golf Club, Deal, in a Mixed Foursomes Stableford competition, June 1957, Mr. G. H. Pickard in playing the fourteenth hole, at which he and his partner were receiving a stroke, holed out from the tee with a full brassie shot, distance 199 yards, and the hole was won in 0.

Hole in One First Recorded

The earliest recorded hole in one was in 1868 at the Open Championship when Tommy Morris (Young Tom) did the eighth hole, 145 yards, Prestwick, in one stroke. This was the first of four open championships won successively by Young Tom.

Holes Halved in One

On Sunday, 9 August 1925, Mr. W. S. Evans and Mr. R. L. Matthews halved the fourteenth hole at Claremont Golf Club, Swinton, in one stroke. The feat is well authenticated, and was witnessed by Messrs. J. Eddie, A. E. Bowen, J. F. Barrett, and W. Freeman, four clubmembers. The normal length of the hole is 133 yards; on this occasion it must have been nearer 140 yards, as the pin was well toward the back of the green. The green was quite clear when the shots were taken, and the four fellow members present were able to see the green clearly. The players immediately called up the four nonparticipants before touching the pin, or approaching nearer the hole, as, realizing at once the tremendous odds against such an occurrence, they desired to have unassailable evidence of the fact. At St. Augustine's, Ramsgate, on 8 May 1925, Miss G. Clutterbuck, St. Augustine's, and Mrs. H. M. Robinson halved the fifteenth hole, 120 yards, in one. At Far Hills, New Jersey, in October 1919, Mr. George Stewart and Mr. Fred Spellmeyer halved the eighteenth hole in one. In September 1929, at Scraptoft, Mr. D. M'Crystel and Mr. T. H. Matthews, two members, both holed out from the tee at the seventeenth. The hole is not visible from the tee, and the players had to drive toward a direction post and also to carry over a dike. The hole measures 243 yards.

Following this achievement at Far Hills, one of the players offered a bet of $10,000 to $1 against the feat's being repeated in his lifetime.

On 31 May 1927 Col. F. G. Crompton (then captain of the Royal Eastbourne Golf Club) halved the thirteenth hole with E. Macey, the assistant professional, in one stroke. The hole measures 175 yards and was played from an elevated tee, from which the whole green and the entire run of the ball could be seen. The players called up one of the groundsmen to take the balls out of the hole before they reached the green, and several other players observed what had happened.

At Colwyn Bay, 1935, Mrs. C. R. Taylor, a former Denbighshire champion, and Mrs. Maurice Jones halved the eighth hole, distance 170 yards, in one.

At Farnham, Surrey, July 1936, T. S. Wilson (Larkhall, Scotland) and J. D. Lyall (Roehampton), playing in singles, both holed their tee strokes at the tenth, 157 yards. After Wilson had holed his shot, Lyall remarked with a smile, "Oh, well, I'll have to do the same thing." And to the astonishment of himself and his opponent, he did.

In April 1968, Mr. Peter Dennett, with a handicap of scratch, was playing against his father, holding a handicap of 22. At the fourteenth hole (173 yards) Mr. Dennett, Jr., holed in one; his father, who is an elderly gentleman, holed in two and with his stroke allowance halved the hole.

At Honor Oak Club, September 1938, R. J. Derwent and J. Rankin holed their tee shots at the eighth, 104 yards.

On 16 July 1939 H. S. Martin and G. E. Mobbs halved the third hole at the Northamptonshire County Golf Club. The hole, 160 yards, is in full view of the players, a flat green and no gather.

In 1948 on the East Course, Wentworth, M. R. Farris and W. B. Poulter, members of the Wentworth Club, and Virginia Water each holed their tee shots at the twelfth, 147 yards.

Holing in One in Foursomes, Four-Ball, and Mixed Foursomes

In 1968 on Sickleholme course, Bamford, in a four-ball match, Tom Gillies and Jack Onions, opponents in the four-ball match, each holed his tee shot at the 167-yard fifth hole. Their respective ages were seventy-five and sixty-seven.

Opposing each other in a four-ball foursome at Turnberry, Ayrshire, on 4 August 1963, Mr. and Mrs. G. Gordon, members of Turnberry Club, each holed their tee shots at the short eleventh hole, the first recorded incident of a husband and wife holing in one at the same green in a foursome.

At Fresh Meadow Country Club in New York, Norman Franke and A. E. Booth playing in a foursome each did the ninth hole in one stroke.

Playing over the Wakefield course, M. N. G. Firth and Dr. J. Wood-Wilson were partners in a four-ball match against Mr. F. J. Nicholls and Mr. M. C. Kay. At the third hole, measuring 150 yards, Mr. Firth and Dr. Wood-Wilson both holed their tee shots. The following day Mr. Nicholls holed his tee shot at the four-teenth, measuring 180 yards.

On 2 May 1957, four members of the Hallowes Golf Club were playing a four-ball match at Renishaw Park Golf Club, near Sheffield. At the second hole Mr. H. J. Marr (handicap 3) was observed to have holed his tee shot of 160 yards with a No. 7 iron. The other members of the four played, Mr. E. Stevenson (handicap 4) being the last to play. On their approaching the hole, a ball was seen trapped by the pin, and it disappeared into the hole as they walked onto the green. On reaching the hole, it was discovered that both Mr. Marr and Mr. Stevenson had holed their tee shots, thus the hole was halved in one.

On 3 September 1954 at the Vestatia's golf course, Birming-ham, Alabama, W. S. Anderson holed his tee shot at the 122-yard seventh hole. The club professional, Jack Murphy, playing in the same four-ball match, said, "I wonder if I could put one right on top of it," as he played his shot. The ball pitched just short of the hole and rolled gently in.

Holing Successive Holes in One

Successive holes in one are rare; successive par-4 holes in one may be classified as near miracles. Mr. N. L. Manley performed the almost incredible feat in September 1964, at Del Valle Country Club, Saugus, California. The par-4 seventh (330 yards) and eighth (290 yards) are both slightly downhill, dogleg holes. Mr. Manley had "aces" at both, en route to a course record of 61 (par 71).

The first recorded example in Britain of a player holing in one stroke at each of two successive holes was achieved on 6 February 1964 at the Walmer and Kingsdown course, Kent. The young assistant professional at that club, Roger Game (age seventeen) holed out with a No. 4 wood at the 244-yard seventh hole, and repeated the feat at the 256-yard eighth hole, using a No. 5 iron.

Early in 1968 two players, one an amateur, holed out in one at two successive holes. The amateur, Henry Ashauer, a public links player, using a driver, aced the 205-yard third hole at Clifton Park Municipal Golf Course in Baltimore and then proceeded with a No. 5 iron to hole out in one at the fourth hole, measuring 127 yards.

A similar feat was achieved by Claude Harmon, winner of the 1948 U.S. Masters and professional at Winged Foot Golf Club, Mamaroneck, New York, who aced the fourth and fifth holes of the par-3 course at the Augusta National Golf Club. The holes measured 60 and 80 yards respectively.

In 1911, at Vancouver Golf and Country Club, Alex Duthie, professional to the Jericho Golf Club, playing in a three-ball match, did two successive holes in one each. The first was a short hole, and Duthie played a full iron; the second was a 200-yard hole, slightly uphill, and Duthie took his brassie off the tee. Corporal Bob Halverty, August 1945, at Recreation Park, Long Beach, California, holed the fifteenth (308 yards) and sixteenth (130 yards) in the same round. Playing over the RAF Changi Golf Course, Singapore, on 13 June 1950, Wing-Commander T. R. Vickers of Wye, Kent, holed the third (100 yards) and fourth (130 yards) in the same round. A No. 6 iron was used for both shots. These are the only recorded instances of two successive holes in one each.

In a Legion Tournament at Woodstock, Ontario, in 1952, Max Banbury of West Vancouver (who was a caddie to Mr. Duthie) performed a similar feat by holing out from the tee at the 180-yard eighth and 245-yard ninth holes, giving him 26 for the nine holes.

Playing in the Gourock Golf Club's Monthly Medal in June

1968, Charles Aairlie holed two successive tee shots. This feat, which is the first recorded in Scotland, was achieved at the fifteenth hole, measuring 162 yards, playing a No. 6 iron, and at the sixteenth hole, measuring 192 yards, with a No. 4 wood.

Holing in One—Greatest Number

The world record for holes in one in a career is thirty-five by Art Wall, Jr., between 1936 and 1966.

C. T. Chevalier has done thirty holes in one, the greatest number of authenticated aces in Britain.

Alex Herd, who died in 1944, did nineteen holes in one. It is a curious thing that when Herd holed for the seventeenth time in one, it was at the seventeenth at Coombe Hill. A curious feat not unconnected with Herd's record is that, subsequent to holing his sixteenth hole in one, Herd was following a match carrying the "jigger" with which he gained some of his holes in one. One of the players asked to try it and immediately holed out in one at the seventeenth, the same hole at which Herd accomplished his seventeenth hole in one.

James Braid, who died in 1950, did eighteen holes in one.

Ernest H. Risebro recorded eighteen holes in one.

Mr. J. T. Smillie, a scratch golfer, Troon, St. Meddan's, has done thirteen holes in one.

The late J. H. Taylor holed in one on ten occasions. His tenth

138

hole in one was achieved at the second hole in his second round in the British Open Championship at Prestwick in 1925. A remarkable circumstance was that at the first hole in this round the professional who was playing with Taylor took 14 to the first hole.

A left-handed golfer, Mr. Fred Francis, has holed out in one five times at the seventh hole (175 yards) of the Cardigan golf course.

An outstanding member of the Mollymook Golf Club, Ulladulla, New South Walles—Mr. E. Latta—held the club championship for the years 1959-60-62-63-64-65. In addition he holed in one five times over a period of seven years from 1958.

Holing in One Twice in the Same Round

Mr. Frank B. Munro, playing in a medal competition over the Blackhill course, Glasgow, in February 1916, did the fifth and seventh holes each in one stroke in the same round. Playing at Worlington, on 3 October 1907, in a three-ball match, Mr. J. Ireland holed the fifth and eighteenth holes each in one stroke. W. E. Macnamara has done two holes at Lahinch in one stroke in the same round. At Acton, on 24 November 1909, Mr. H. C. Josecelyne holed the third (175 yards) and fourteenth (115 yards) in one stroke in the same round. At Painswick, on 31 August 1923, J. H. Busson, when sixteen years old, playing with

J. W. Musty at Gloucester did the sixth hole (100 yards) and the seventeenth hole (260 yards) in one stroke. Cyril Davey, assistant professional at Westgate-on-Sea, in 1927, did the thirteenth (163 yards) and sixteenth (120 yards) in one in the same round. R. Houliston, playing with the captain of the club at Crichton in Dumfries in 1928, did the fourth (151 yards), and the twelfth (148 yards), in one in the same round. Fred Cox, at Pollard's Hill, on 11 November 1929, did the first and seventh holes (each 146 yards) in one stroke. Major R. A. Chrystal, on 29 October 1931, did the eleventh (154 yards) and fifteenth (105 yards) at Callander in one stroke. Mike Brady at the Siasconset Country Club, Massachusetts, on 4 September 1917 (Labor Day), did the sixth and thirteenth holes in one. Mr. Maurice Watson, a member of the Northcliffe Golf Club, Shipley, holed out in one, twice in the same round, on the Northcliffe Golf Course on 29 April 1934. The two holes were the eighth (145 yards) and the twelfth (120 yards). In February 1936 James Sherlock, at Aldeburgh, did the fourth (130 yards) and the seventeenth (140 yards) in the one round in one stroke. These brought Sherlock's total of ones to eleven.

There are many other examples from all over the world. In America, in the qualifying round for the U.S. Open Championship at Plum Hollow Golf Club, Detroit, on 31 May 1949, Ray Maguire, professional at the Birmingham Country Club, holed out from the tee at the 205-yard fifth, and repeated at the 164-yard fourteenth. It was in his second round.

Holing in One—Longest Holes

Although he is only 5 ft. 6 in. high, weighs 165 lbs., and wears glasses, Bob Mitera, twenty-one-year-old American student, claims the world's record for the longest hole in one. Playing over the appropriately named Miracle Hill course at Omaha, on 7 October 1965, Bob holed his drive at the tenth hole, 444 yards long. The ground slopes sharply downhill, and the astonished Bob was further aided by a strong following wind and (he admits) a lot of luck.

In March 1961, Lou Kretlow holed his tee shot at the 427-yard sixteenth hole at Lake Hefner Course, Oklahoma City.

Another very long hole accomplished in one was the ninth hole at Hillcrest Golf Club, Winston-Salem, North Carolina, by Mr. Cardwell. The hole (425 yards) is a par-4. The authenticity of this feat was vouched for by Mr. Ken C. Abels, the manager of the Hillcrest Golf Club.

A ball driven by a driving machine holed out in one at the 435-yard first hole at Hermitage Country Club, Richmond, Virginia.

The longest hole in one authenticated in Great Britain is the fifth at Tankersley Park, near Sheffield, length 380 yards, where, in 1961, Mr. David Hulley holed a drive.

The next-longest hole in one recorded in Great Britain was at Phoenix Golf Club, Rotherham, 1957, when D. J. Palmer holed out in one with his tee shot from the first hole, distance 345

yards. On 24 September 1928 George Kirby, the local professional at Stoneham, Southampton, at the ninth hole, which measures 340 yards, holed out with his drive. Other notable holes done in one are the eighteenth at Low Laithes, Ossett (Yorkshire), 1953, by Mr. Harry Haley, Leeds, distance 334 yards; the eighteenth at Merton Park, which Mr. R. R. Burton, formerly Oxford, holed with his tee shot on 21 May 1920, distance 330 yards; the seventeenth at Henley-on-Thames by Mr. A. C. Ladd in 1912, distance 330 yards; the fifteenth at Eastbourne Downs, distance 325 yards, by Mr. A. Coomber; the ninth at Scarborough, 300 yards, by J. F. Wilson; the eighth at Lethamhill, 300 yards, by J. O. Stevenson; the tenth at Moortown, 299 yards, by Horace Fulford; the fourth at Bathgate, 295 yards, by George G. Grant; ninth at St. Andrews by J. F. Anderson when the hole was 277 yards; tenth at Hartsbourne, 265 yards, by Keith Gilbert.

The longest recorded hole in one by a woman was that accomplished in September 1949 by Marie Robie—the 393-yard first hole at Furnace Brook Course, Wollaston, Massachusetts.

Holing in One and Holing a Full Shot to Win a Championship or Match

Ending a match by holing in one or with a full shot, is infrequent enough to be worthy of individually placing on the record here.

As an example of a remarkable recovery with the climax of delivering the almost unanswerable hole in one, we record the match in the first round of the Oxford and Cambridge Society's President's Putter at Rye, January 1937, between P. H. F. White, the West of England Champion, 1936, and Leonard Crawley. Crawley was two up and six to play. White won the next three to take the lead, and he holed the seventeenth (230 yards) with his tee shot to win by 2 and 1. Willie Park, in 1898, at Troon, in the second half of his match for £200 against Willie Fernie, holed a full brassie shot at the seventh hole—the sixty-first of the match—to win, the most dramatic ending to a first-class professional match.

In the final Tain Open Amateur Tournament, 8 August 1935, R. F. Sinclair, Golspie, standing two holes up with three to play on F. L. Levick, Eastwood, holed his tee shot at the sixteenth hole, distance 135 yards, and thus finished the match. This is the only recorded case of the final of an important tournament being brought to a conclusion by one of the competitors holing in one.

Dick Mayer, U.S. professional, won $50,000 for scoring a hole in one in the Palm Springs Tournament of 1962. This was the third successive year the feat had been performed in this tournament. The sponsors insure against "aces" with Lloyds of London.

Two Australian golfers, John Wise and Glen Hutton, influenced by the fact that two tennis players had signed a contract for a 100-match series, agreed to play a similar golf series limited to ten matches per year. In 1967, Hutton won the 99th match to lead in the series. In the 100th match, Wise holed in one at the last hole to win the hole, the match, and to end the series all square.

Holing in One—Curious Incidents

Harry Vardon, who scored the greatest number of victories in the Open Championship, only once did a hole in one. That was in 1903 at Mundesley, Norfolk, where Vardon was convalescing from a long illness.

Walter Hagen, one of the greatest and most colorful golfers of all time, did only one hole in one in his long career. It was at Worcester, Massachusetts, in 1925.

Mrs. Harold J. (Ginny) Leyes, 1722 East Cedar Street, South Bend, Indiana, at 1 P.M., 21 July 1966, playing at Morris Park Golf Club, holed out in one at par-3 hole No. 9—distance 172 yards—with her driver. At about 2 P.M. the same day, her husband holed out in one at the same hole with his No. 3 iron.

Having watched Paul Hahn play a trick shot while kneeling, on his knees, Jim Hadderer, of Elgin, Illinois, a lad of sixteen, tried the same "gag" at a 190-yard hole at the Wing Park course in 1965. He improved on Hahn's performance by popping the ball into the hole in one.

Lt. David Butler holed out a 7-iron tee shot on the 197-yard eighteenth at Brady Club, California. His ball hit a wire over the green and dropped into the hole. And Bobby Vollmer, of El Paso, Texas, saw his drive at a short hole at the Anthony Country Club bounce off a lizard on the green and run into the hole.

146

When he holed in one at the 105-yard fourteenth hole at Tahoe Paradise Course, in the Harrah Invitational Tournament in 1965, Dick Kolbus, from Oakland, California, won an $18,500 Rolls-Royce car.

In the Army Golf Championship at Prestwick, 30 April 1930, Captain E. D. Stevenson started by taking a 10 on the first hole, and he finished the round by holing in one stroke at the eighteenth.

After having holed a No. 7 iron shot for an eagle-2 at the tenth hole on the Old Course, St. Andrews, Councillor C. M. Davidson was challenged by one of his opponents to hole his tee shot at the next hole—163 yards. He accepted the challenge and put the ball into the hole with a No. 3 iron.

One hour before he retired as captain of the Royal Guernsey Golf Club, Channel Islands, Mr. R. J. Mahy (handicap 1) holed out in one at the eighteenth hole while playing in a medal competition on 12 March 1964. This was his first "ace"—a thrilling climax with his final stroke as captain of the club.

Two holes in one with an interval of fifty-five years between— that is the boast of Major A. Gordon Taylor, Kenilworth, Cape Town. His first ace was at the sixth hole of Royal Dornoch course in 1906; his second at the seventeenth hole of the Royal Cape course in 1961. On another occasion at the sixth at Dornoch, his ball struck his opponent's on the green and knocked it into the hole for a score of one.

A father and son, Leslie and Keith Pickles, members of Bradley Hall Club, Halifax, had holes in one within half an hour of each other on a day in September 1964. Keith had his ace at the short fourth, and later, as he passed his father on the course, halted to describe his feat. Leslie, the father, waiting to play to the second hole, then drove and emulated his son's achievement—to the consternation of all concerned.

Within half an hour of each other on 6 May 1909, Mr. Thorp Whitaker and his son, Mr. C. T. Whitaker, playing in separate matches, got the second hole on West Bowling Course (Bradford) in one stroke. The hole, which is not a "blind" one, is only a mashie shot onto the green. On 10 May 1910, Mr. A. J. Gardner holed the sixteenth at Saltford Links, Bristol, in one stroke, and Mrs. S. Pim-Jackson, in the immediately succeeding match, also holed the sixteenth in one.

Dr. Tucker, New Orleans, Louisiana, 1936, put his name down for a hole-in-one golf tournament. After doing so he walked out to the contest hole—160 yards—and hit the ball with an iron. The ball trickled into the hole. Elated, Dr. Tucker rushed back to the clubhouse, only to find that the competition was not due to begin until two weeks later.

Miss Gertrude Lawrence, the distinguished actress, when playing golf for the first time, holed in one with her first tee shot.

Joe Kirkwood holed in one on eleven occasions including one when doing a Newsreel Movie Camera feature at the fifth (168 yards), Sea Island, Georgia, and another when he was performing trick shots off the face of a watch at the first (268 yards), Cedar Rapids, Iowa.

Mr. J. A. Brown, a well-known Border golfer, had an unusual hole in one when playing over the Torwoodlee course at Galashiels in September 1953. At the third hole (160 yards), his ball went straight off his No. 6 iron into the hole without touching either the fairway or the green and became jammed between the side of the cup and the flag.

A remarkable hole in one was done by Mr. F. H. Byrde in playing over the New Galloway Golf Course in 1926. His drive to the fourth hole (190 yards) went over the wall out of bounds, and the ball, striking a rock, rebounded on to the green, 50 yards away, and found the hole.

As for the "unlucky Friday the 13th" superstition: Tommy (Thunder) Bolt, the picturesque American pro—former U.S. Open Champion—scored his thirteenth hole in one at Friday, 13 January 1961, while playing in the San Diego Open.

At Cuddington, Banstead Downs, 18 March 1924, H. E. Brown and H. L. Sim, playing to the eighth hole, one ball holed out and the other was on the edge of the hole. The players were playing new balls of the same make and identical in every respect, and neither could tell who had done the hole in one.

Playing over Buckpool Course, Buckie, in August 1969, a local player, George Murray, holed his tee shot at the 196-yard sixth hole. Next day, during a round with two other friends, he repeated the feat at the same hole and almost at the same time as on the previous day.

There have been numerous instances where a player has holed out in one and his opponent in two, and instances of players holing out off their tee shot at a hole other than the hole played at. In this category the most remarkable is that of R. Slater at Blackpool, who teed up on the first tee and completed the course in one stroke. His drive struck the flagstaff which stands between the eighteenth green and the first fairway, ricochetted to the eighteenth green, and dropped into the eighteenth hole: First tee to eighteenth hole in one stroke, the only record of such an incident.

John Turtle, of the Mount Herbert Club, Hawkes Bay, New Zealand, holed in one at the sixth hole on his home links on three consecutive Sundays, the first three Sundays of July 1934. The hole measured only 95 yards, but the position of it, on a practically level green, was shifted each week, and on the third occasion of holing in one the ball dropped into the hole—three 1's at the same hole within fifteen days.

G. M. White, professional at Coxmoor, Nottinghamshire, on 15 December 1948 was at the third at Coxmoor (303 yards), a dogleg over a spinney. There were two players putting on the green, one of whom had struck his ball toward the hole when White's drive came onto the green, struck this player's ball a glancing blow, and went into the hole. It was White's first hole in one.

Arthur Powell, Muskerry, Cork, sliced his drive to the ninth hole out of bounds. The ball hit the roof of a cottage, bounced back to the fairway, ran to the green, and holed out. The distance, tee to green, was 265 yards.

R. H. Locke, at Pannal, 3 July 1937, at 10 P.M., holed his tee shot at the fifteenth hole, distance 220 yards. It was bright moonlight. The only known instance of holing in one at such a time.

There are known cases of dreaming of holing in one and actually doing so. At Rochford, Essex, one Sunday morning a player said he dreamed that he had done the tenth hole in one. Fantastic bets were laid against his actually doing so. A number of members went out to see him play the hole; to their amazement he holed out in one. The old tenth at Rochford is still known as the "dream hole."

E. C. B. Shannon, Lloyds Bank, Bombay, 8 December 1938, was having slow motion pictures taken of his shots at the eleventh hole (180 yards), Peshawar Golf Club, Northern India, when he holed in one. Slow motion photography and holing in one, a unique incident.

R. R. Smiley, Goldsboro, North Carolina, in 1939 scored a hole in one backward! Teeing off on the thirteenth, he badly sliced his ball. It landed into the hole on the eleventh green—and stayed there.

One of the most astounding holes in one was made by Bob Gaared at a Los Angeles golf course in December 1950. At the second hole (425 yards), his tee shot went out of bounds onto the road which runs beside the fairway. The ball bounced on the road and landed in a passing truck which was going toward the second green. The driver stopped his vehicle at the green, and not knowing anything about the rules of golf, obliged Gaared by putting the ball in the hole. Gaared considered he had done the hole in one—as he had—but the committee ruled at the end of the round that he had gone out of bounds and ought to have returned to the tee and played a second drive.

Miss Maureen Sharpe, a Bangor schoolmistress, playing with Miss Gladys Broxton, at St. Dieniol, Bangor, on 7 May 1954, holed her tee shot at the third hole. On the following day, 8 May 1954, once more playing with Miss Broxton but in a foursome, she again holed the third in one stroke.

D. C. Murray, a member of Gullane Golf Club, took on a wager that he would not do a hole in one within a year. The odds were a case of whiskey to a cigar. The bet was made on a Saturday in August 1955, and in a four-baller with Muirfield members the very next day he holed the thirteenth on the No. 1 Gullane course in one.

Playing over Rickmansworth course at Easter 1960, Mrs. A. E. (Paddy) Martin achieved a remarkable sequence of aces. On Good Friday she sank her tee shot at the third hole (125 yards). The next day, using the same ball and the same No. 8 iron, at the same hole, she scored another 1. And on the Monday (same ball, same club, same hole) she again holed out from the tee. Three singles in four days at the same hole by an 18-handicap player must surely be a world record.

Ian Booker, an eighteen-year-old member of Cuddington Golf Club, averaged a hole in one every twelve weeks during the fifteen months prior to April 1968. His aces were all achieved at Cuddington's five different short holes. His sequence, commemorated by a special plaque in the clubhouse, was as follows: 148 yards (9 iron); 142 yards (7 iron); 171 yards (7 iron); 162 yards (7 iron); and 195 yards (2 iron).

Oldest and Youngest Holing in One

Mrs. Fred Reeves (age seventy-one) of Midland, Michigan, watched golf on television and thought it looked easy. So she borrowed a few clubs, went out to a little nine-hole course, and shot the third hole (90 yards) in one stroke. She completed the nine holes in 48—or 21 over par.

T. S. South, a member of Highcliffe Castle Golf Club, holed the seventh, 110 yards on that course, in 1952, at the age of ninety-one—the oldest recorded golfer to do this feat.

The second oldest golfer to do this feat was H. A. Clear, who did the sixth hole (135 yards) at Yelverton Golf Club, Yelverton, Devon, in one stroke, on 8 October 1956, at the age of eighty-eight.

Sharing second place is Mr. C. J. Wain, of North Hants Golf Club, Fleet, who holed his tee shot at the fifteenth hole (143 yards) on 24 August 1969, at the age of eighty-eight.

In 1954, Mr. George Borrowbridge, Madison, Wisconsin, an eighty-two-year-old golfer, had the first hole in one of his lengthy golfing career at the Burr Oaks golf course.

General Eisenhower early in 1968 holed the thirteenth at Seven Lakes Country Club in one. It was his first ace, and thirteen was not an unlucky number. He was seventy-seven.

At the age of six years, one month, and seven days, Tommy Moore holed in one at the 145-yard fourth hole at Woodbrier Course, Martinsville, West Virginia, on 8 March 1968. He repeated this feat before reaching the age of seven years.

When he was only six years and three months old, Joe Dobson, Jr., holed in one at the 155-yard fourth hole at Meadowlark course, Enid, Oklahoma, in 1958.

Peter Toogood, the son of A. H. Toogood, professional to Kingston Beach Golf Club, when eight years old did the seventh hole at Kingston (110 yards) in one stroke.

Beverley J. Pyke, age fifteen, on 30 August 1950, holed the eighth (135 yards) at Runcorn, in one, witnessed by the club professional. On 8 September he did the same hole again in one, witnessed by two junior members with whom he was playing. A record for a boy of his age, to do the same hole in one twice within ten days.

Holing in One—Odds Against

At the Wanderers Club, Johannesburg in January 1951, forty-nine amateurs and professionals each played three balls at a hole 146 yards long. Of the 147 balls hit, the nearest was by Koos de Beer, professional at Reading Country Club, which finished 10½ inches from the hole. Harry Bradshaw, the Irish professional who was touring with the British team in South Africa, touched the pin with his second shot, but the ball rolled on and stopped 3 feet 2 inches from the cup.

A competition on similar lines was held in 1951 in New York when 1,400 players who had done a hole in one held a competition over several days at short holes on three New York golf courses. Each player was allowed a total of five shots, so 7,000 shots were hit. No player holed in one, and the nearest ball finished 3½ inches from the hole.

A further illustration of the element of luck in holing in one is derived from an effort by Harry Gonder, an American professional, who in 1940 stood for 16 hours 25 minutes and hit 1,817 balls trying to do a 160-yard hole in one. He had two official witnesses and caddies to tee and retrieve the balls and count the strokes. His first fifty shots took 15 minutes; his 86th shot finished 15 inches short; after playing 941 shots he stopped for food; his 996th shot hit the pin and bounced 3 inches away; at 8:10 P.M.

his 1,162nd shot halted 6 inches short, and his 1,184th shot missed by 3 inches; at midnight he struck the 1,600th shot. By then there was a blister on his hand; and after passing 1,700 his hands began to throb, and he could feel each shot up to the elbow. His 1,750th shot struck the hole and came out, and his 1,756th shot did exactly the same thing but stopped an inch from the hole. At 2:40 A.M. his 1,817th shot stopped 10 feet from the pin, and he then gave up his effort to hole in one.

Cyril Wagner, another American professional, got a hole in one in 805 shots. The odds might be reckoned 1,500-2,000 to 1. If a proficient player, who from the tee had the power to play a shot which would cover the top of the pin, stood continuously punching balls to that number, he ought to succeed in doing a hole in one.

Holed in One—And Lost or Gave Up

Mr. Robert Clark, an Edinburgh printer and the author of one of the rare works on golf, was playing at Musselburgh in 1870 in a foursome, and as it was almost dark when the game was finished there was much searching for Mr. Clark's ball when the players had walked from the tee to the green. They looked for it everywhere, and Mr. Clark and his partner all the more anxiously since the match depended on this last hole. At last with much regret, they had to give the ball up as lost, and the match as lost with it; and when this irrevocable step had been taken, the ball was found in the hole itself! This is not the only time on record, extraordinary as it may be, when a match was lost because the loser accomplished what in its way is the greatest feat in golf. At Reigate a lady, playing in a stroke competition, did a short hole in one, but as the hole was not in sight from the tee, she did not know it. After searching for the ball and not finding it, she went back and played another, and only discovered that she had holed her first tee shot on holing out her second ball. The Rules of Golf Committee were asked if her score in the competition should be 1 or 5 and they decided, "When the player abandoned the search for the first ball it became a 'lost ball' and the second ball played became the ball 'in play.'" The USGA disagreed and ruled that her score was 1 as the play of the hole was completed when the player holed the original ball. The Royal and Ancient afterward adopted this ruling.

On Roehampton Course, late in an evening of July 1964, Bill Carey drove to the short seventh green. In the gathering darkness he could not find his ball, and conceded the hole to his opponent, Edgar Winter, whose drive had stopped on the lip of the hole. Carey's ball was then found in the hole—his first hole in one—but, as he had already conceded the hole, he could not claim a win.

In June 1951, Mr. Mark Sutherland did the 160-yard twelfth hole on the Merchants of Edinburgh Course in one, but lost the hole. Mr. Sutherland's first tee shot appeared to go out of bounds and, playing a provisional ball, he holed in one. On inspection, however, his first ball was discovered in bounds and holing it out, Mr. Sutherland took four to his opponent's two.

Holes in One—Endowed

There are five holes in the world where you do get paid for achieving a one. The first is if you happen to do it at either the Easter, Whitsuntide, or Autumn meetings at the "island hole" on the course of the Royal Ashdown Forest Club in Sussex. It is an excellent hole, and a visitor to the club, Mr. J. Lionel Redpath, who played it on one occasion fell so much in love with it that he endowed it with a sum of £5, the accumulated interest on the sum to go to the competitor at any of the meetings named who should do it in one. Ever since the endowment was made, the interest has been growing and growing, and nobody had qualified for it. The hole has been done several times in one but not in a competition. On one occasion when a member played in a competition in the morning and in a second round in the afternoon, he did the "island hole" in one, but he could not receive the interest as, to do so, the hole must be done in a competition. At the Druid Hills Club, United States, a similar fund exists for anyone doing the eighth hole in one stroke.

The fourth hole (156 yards) at the Exeter Golf and Country

Club has been endowed with £25 war stock, the interest to accumulate and to be paid to any member doing a hole in one in a competition. In 1953, Mrs. Edith Peters achieved the feat and won the accumulated interest amounting to £17 15s. 10d. The interest accumulates for the next occasion. Under similar conditions the tenth (194 yards) at the same course has recently been endowed with the sum of £20.

The fifth, or spinney, hole at Sleaford Golf Club was endowed with £5 by Mr. P. G. Morgan in 1951, the interest going to any golfer who does the hole in one in a recognized competition. Mr. Morgan, who once holed his tee shot at the spinney (110 yards) was a member of the Sleaford Golf Club for forty years, and the endowment was to commemorate both events.

Holing in One in the Championships

The unparalleled achievement of twice holing in one in a championship match was accomplished by Mr. Eric Fiddian, Stourbridge, in the final of the Irish Open Championship over thirty-six holes at Newcastle, County Down, on 23 September 1933. Mr. Fiddian, who was Boy Champion in 1927 and English Champion in 1932, was opposed to Mr. Jack McLean. In the first round Mr. Fiddian did the seventh hole (128 yards) in one stroke, and in the second round he did the fourteenth hole (205 yards), also in one stroke. These remarkable strokes did not carry

Mr. Fiddian to victory, for he was defeated by 3 and 2.

Other authenticated incidents of holing in one in championships are:

1868: Tom Morris, Jr. (Young Tommy), in the first of the four British Open Championships which he won, did the eighth hole at Prestwick (145 yards) in one stroke.

1878: Jamie Anderson, the seventeenth at Prestwick. The circumstances were extraordinary. Anderson was playing the next to the last hole, and though it seemed then that he was winning easily, it turned out afterward that if he had not taken this hole in one stroke he would very likely have lost. Anderson was just about to make his tee shot when Andy Stuart (winner of the first Irish Open Championship in 1892), who was acting as marker to Anderson, remarked that he was standing outside the teeing ground and that, if he played the stroke from there, he would be disqualified. Anderson quietly picked up his ball and teed it in a proper place. Then he holed in one. The circumstances prior to this feat were almost extraordinary. At the "burn" hole, Anderson, after recovering from a bunker, holed a full iron shot. At the next hole he ran down a 15-yard putt, and at the second last, the short hole at that time, he holed in one. He won the British Open Championship by one stroke. It is the most dramatic sequence of events in the winning of the championship.

1885: Mr. A. F. Macfie, in the fourth round of the initial competition at Hoylake for the British Amateur Championship, holed the fourteenth, or "rushes," hole in one. His opponent, Mr. W. M.

deZoete, had what is termed a "sitting two." Mr. Macfie won the tie by two holes and finally won the championship.

1906: R. Johnston, North Berwick, competing in the Open Championship, did the fourteenth hole at Muirfield in one. Johnston played with only one club throughout—an adjustable-head club.

1910: Mrs. Wingfield Stratford, in her tie with Miss E. Grant Suttie, in the first round of the Ladies' Championship, did the third hole at Westward Ho! in one.

1921: Jock Hutchison, in his first round in the British Open Championship at St. Andrews, did the eighth hole in one. At the ninth hole his drive was dead on the hole, and a spectator rushing forward pulled out the flagpin. The ball jumped over the hole, and many onlookers thought that if the spectator had not interfered Hutchison might have achieved the unique feat in the championship of a second and successive hole in one. In his play in this championship Hutchison actually hit the pin three times with full shots. Hutchison tied for the championship and won on the play-off against Mr. Roger Wethered. In the championship the amateur actually played one shot less than Hutchison, for he trod on his ball at the fourteenth hole in the third round and was penalized a stroke. Wethered went forward to study the line of putt and retired slowly toward his ball, keeping his eye on the line, and he knocked the ball with his foot before he realized he had reached it.

1925: J. H. Taylor, in his second round in the British Open

Championship at Prestwick, did the second hole in one stroke. Mr. Murdoch, of Troon Municipal, who played with Taylor, took 14 at the first hole, and it is a championship record that the third highest score for a hole in the Open Championship and the lowest possible should be made at successive holes in the same round and by competitors playing together.

J. H. Taylor had another experience of a high-scoring partner when competing for the British Open Championship at St. Andrews in 1895. Playing to the "road hole," the formidable seventeenth, Taylor, who was the reigning champion, played safely along the wall, not venturing to go over the stationmaster's garden, then a brassie, a three-quarter mashie, and two putts; he got a par-5. His partner, too strong with his third, went onto the road and took 13. Taylor won the championship for the second time, and in 1913 he won his fifth Open Championship.

1930: Mr. Maurice McCarthy, Jr., in the qualifying stroke competition of the U.S. Amateur Championship at Merion did a hole in one. Mr. McCarthy tied for the last place and qualified for the championship in the play-off.

1931: Leo Diegel did the thirteenth hole (146 yards), in the U.S. Open Championship, at Inverness Course, Toledo, Ohio, 4 July.

Tony Jacklin, in winning the 1967 Masters Tournament at Royal St. Geoge's, Sandwich, did the sixteenth hole in one. His ace has an exceptional place in the records, for it was seen by millions on television, the ball in view in its flight till it went into the hole in his final round of 64.

Record Ties

In the third round of the Professional Match Play Championship at Walton Heath, 18 September 1952, Fred Daly defeated Alan (Tiger) Poulton at the thirtieth hole. This is a record in a professional tournament in the British Isles. The previous record was in 1904, when Willie Fernie beat James Braid at the twenty-seventh hole in the Irvine Professional Tournament at Bogside.

In the U.S. Open Championship at Toledo, Ohio, in July 1931, G. Von Elm and Billy Burke twice tied for the title. Each returned scores of 292. On the first replay both finished in 149 for 36 holes, but on second replay Burke won with a score of 148 against 149. This is a record tie in a national open championship.

In the semifinal round of the Scottish Foursome Tournament at Dunbar, 25 September 1937, Ayr Academy beat Pollock at the twenty-seventh hole, a record in first-class tournament in Scotland.

Mr. C. A. Palmer beat Mr. Lionel Munn at the twenty-eighth hole at Sandwich 1908. This is the record tie of the British Amateur Championship.

Lionel Munn was engaged in two other extended ties in the British Amateur Championship. At Muirfield, 1932, in the semifinal, he was defeated by John de Forest, the ultimate winner, at the twenty-sixth hole, and at St. Andrews, 1936, in the second round he was defeated by J. L. Mitchell, again at the twenty-sixth hole. Munn's record of marathon ties is unique in the history of the British Amateur Championship.

G. H. Grimwade (Melbourne and Cambridge) beat R. H. Oppenheimer (Harrow and Oxford) at the forty-first hole, 30 March 1927, in the Oxford-Cambridge match. The match was thirty-six holes. A record tie in the interuniversity match.

In the U.S. Amateur Championship, at Merion, 1930, Maurice M'Carthy, Jr., beat George Von Elm at the twenty-eighth hole— ten extra holes. This is the record tie in the U.S. Amateur Championship.

In the fifth round, Amateur Championship, Troon, 1938, Hector Thomson and S. L. McKinlay halved every hole from the eighth to the nineteenth. Thomson won at the twentieth.

The two finalists in a woman's tournament at Paterson, New Jersey, eventually decided at the one hundred sixth hole. Mrs. Edwin Labaugh, after eighty-eight extra holes, was the winner, and the score was duly set down in the club records as "one up, 106th."

Exceptionally prolonged matches have taken place where the conditions of a competition provide that, in the event of a tie, three extra holes, nine extra holes, or another round should be played.

In June 1949, Cary Middlecoff, holder of the U.S. Open Championship, and Lloyd Mangrum, in the Open Tournament at Detroit, tied with scores of 273. They played eleven extra holes without being able to settle matters, and then agreed to share the prize money.

In the final of the Irish Open Amateur Championship at Rosses Point in 1950, J. B. Carr beat R. C. Ewing at the fortieth hole, a record for the final of this championship.

In the final of the American Amateur Championship at Minneapolis in 1950, Sam Urzetta beat Frank R. Stranahan at the thirty-ninth hole, a record for the final of this championship, which is over thirty-six holes.

In the fourth round of the American Ladies' Championship at Atlanta in 1950, Miss Mae Murray, the eventual runner-up, beat Miss Fay Crocker, Uruguay, at the twenty-seventh hole, in a scheduled eighteen-hole round. This is a record tie for this championship.

In the German Open Championship at Krefeld in 1954, A. D. Locke, South Africa, and D. J. Rees, Great Britain, tied with 279 for the four rounds. Another eighteen holes were played, and this resulted in another tie at 69. It was decided to play nine more holes, and Locke became the titleholder with 37 strokes to Rees's 38.

Record Championship Victories

In the Amateur Championship at Muirfield, 1920, Captain Carter, an Irish golfer, defeated an American entrant by 10 and 8. This is the only instance where a player won every hole in an Amateur Championship.

In the Boys' Amateur Championship at Fulwell, London, 1930, W. Hancock, Welbeck Abbey Club, won his first round 10 and 8. In this championship a boy won the first nine holes, and, to avoid inflicting an 10 and 8 victory, he deliberately drove his tee shot to the tenth into an adjacent wood and gave the hole to his opponent.

In the final of the Canadian Ladies' Championship at Rivermead, Ottawa, 1921, Miss Cecil Leitch defeated Miss Mollie McBride by 17 and 15. Miss Leitch only lost one hole in the match, the ninth. She was 14 up at the end of the first round, and only three holes were necessary in the second round, Miss Leitch winning them all. She won eighteen holes out of twenty-one played, lost one, and halved two.

In the final of the French Ladies' Open Championship at Le Touquet, 23 June 1927, Mlle de la Chaume (St. Cloud) defeated Mrs. Alex Johnston (Moor Park) by 15 and 14, the largest victory in a European golf championship.

At Prestwick, 1934, Mr. W. Lawson Little, Presidio, San Francisco, defeated James Wallace, Troon, Portland, by 14 up and 13 in the final of the Amateur Championship, the record victory in the Amateur Championship. Little did the first nine holes in 33 and was 6 up. He did the second nine in 33, and at the end of the round he was 11 up. Little's figures for the five holes in the second round were 3, 3, 4, 3, 3. He won three of the holes in winning by 14 and 13. Wallace never won a single hole, which was a record occurrence in the 36-hole final of the Amateur Championship. For the twenty-three holes played, Little's score was 82.

Remarkable Recoveries

There were two remarkable recoveries in the Walker Cup match. In 1930 at Sandwich, J. A. Stout, Great Britain, who went round in 68 was 4 up at the end of the first round against Donald Moe. Stout started in the second round, 3, 3, 3, and was 7 up. He was still 7 up with 13 to play. Moe, who went round in 67, won back the seven holes to draw level at the seventeenth green. At the eighteenth or thirty-sixth of the match, Moe, after a long drive, placed his iron shot within 3 feet of the hole and won the match by one hole.

In 1936 at Pine Valley, George Voigt and Harry Girvan, for America, were 7 up with 11 to play against Alec Hill and Cecil Ewing. The British pair drew equal at the seventeenth hole, or the thirty-fifth of the match, and the last hole was halved.

In the 1965 Piccadilly Match-Play Championship, Gary Player beat Tony Lema after being 7 down with 17 to play.

Bobby Cruickshank, the old Edinburgh player, had an extraordinary recovery in a thirty-six-hole match in a USPGA Championship, for he defeated Al Watrous after being 11 down with 12 to play.

Remarkable Shots

Remarkable shots are to be numbered as the grains of sand; around every nineteenth hole legends are recalled of astounding shots. One shot is commemorated by a memorial tablet at the seventeenth hole at the Royal Lytham and St. Anne's Club. It was made by R. T. Jones in the final round of the British Open Championship in 1926. He was partnered by Al Watrous, another American player. They had been running neck and neck and, at the end of the third round, Watrous was leading Jones with 215 against 217. On the seventeenth, the seventy-first of the Championship, Jones had drawn level. He drove into a sandy lie in broken ground. Watrous reached the green with his second. Jones took a mashie-iron (the equivalent to a No. 4 iron today) and hit a magnificent shot to the green to get his 4. This remarkable recovery unnerved Watrous, who three-putted, and Jones, getting another 4 at the last hole against 5, won his first Open Championship with 291 against Watrous's 293. The tablet is at the spot where Jones played his second shot.

Arnold Palmer, playing in the second round of the Australian Wills Masters tournament at Melbourne, in October 1964, hooked his second shot at the ninth hole high into the fork of a gum tree. Climbing 20 feet up the tree, Palmer, with the head of his No. 1 iron reversed, played a "hammer" stroke and knocked the ball to the ground 10 feet away, followed by a brilliant chip to the green and a putt.

Johnny Farrell, in the Ryder Cup Match at Moortown in 1929, at the last hole pulled his second shot behind the clubhouse, and the ball finished among a collection of boxes and crates. Farrell walked backward and forward, round the clubhouse to the green and back to his ball, and then played a niblick shot over the clubhouse. The ball landed so close to the pin that he holed the putt and got a par-4.

Lew Worsham in the "World's Championship" at Tam O'Shanter, 9 August 1953, at the last hole from a distance of 135 yards, holed a wedge shot for a 2 at the 410-yard hole. This incredible shot made him the winner by one stroke and gave him the greatest jackpot in golf at that time, $25,000. The difference between the first and third prizes was equivalent to $12,000.

Slowest Rounds

Slow-motion golf has marred many championships, and notorious tortoises have been known to take three and a half hours in a championship tie. The slowest important match was when Henry Cotton and R. A. Whitcombe played Bobby Locke and Sid Brews at Walton Heath, 1938, for a stake of £500 a side. Locke, who was engaging in his first important professional match in

Great Britain, was ultracareful, and the marshaling of the crowd —there were 5,000 spectators present during the second round— caused many delays, sometimes as much as ten minutes being required for the players to leave one green and play off the next tee. The first round took three hours forty minutes and the second round four hours fifteen minutes. Cotton and Whitcombe won by 2 and 1. Locke, although on the defeated side, played phenomenal golf. He went round in 63. Walton Heath tees were far extended, and it was a cruel test. In the Scottish Amateur Championship, 1922, at St. Andrews, a competitor was deplorably slow; and in one match his opponent, hoping to shame the sloth to quicken his play, brought to the links a camp bed, which was carried round by others who had been playing in the championship. The camp bed was placed at the side of each green, and while the tortoise crawled about studying the line of the putt, his opponent reclined on the bed and nonchalantly observed the antics of his rival. The attempt to secure a speed-up was unsuccessful, and the tortoise was even more deliberate in his play.

In the 1966 USPGA National Team Championship Arnold Palmer and Jack Nicklaus (presumably paired with two others) took five hours and fifty minutes in the third round.

The slowest stroke-play tournament round on record was one of five hours fifteen minutes by Sam Snead and Ben Hogan versus Stan Leonard and Al Balding in the Canada Cup contest at Wentworth in 1956. This was a four-ball medal round.

Wooden Ball Championship

During the 1939–45 war there was a famine in golf balls, and wooden balls were fashioned, especially in remote countries, so that golfers could get a round of sorts. A Wooden Golf Ball Championship was played at Potchefstroom, South Africa. The winner was A. A. Horne, of Potchefstroom (90), and the winner of the Women's Championship Mrs. Corneille (116). The best results from the wooden balls were attained by teeing up for every shot and using a brassie or spoon, with an approaching iron and putter. By facing the wooden clubs with about 3/16ths of an inch of balata belting or rubber insertion packing, distances of 200 yards were attained, and the life of the ball increased.

1939–45 War Rules

During the Battle of Britain, players on golf courses were attacked by German bombers. To meet the conditions, the following rules were written by Major G. L. Edsell, secretary of St. Mellon's Golf and Country Club, and generally adopted:

1. Players are asked to collect bomb and shell splinters from the fairways to save these causing damage to the mowers.
2. In competitions, during gunfire or while bombs are falling,

players may take cover without penalty for ceasing play.

3. The positions of known delayed-action bombs are marked by red and white flags placed at reasonably, but not guaranteed, safe distances from the bombs.

4. Shell and/or bomb splinters on the greens may be removed without penalty. On the fairways or in bunkers within a club's length of a ball, they may be moved without penalty and no penalty shall be incurred if a ball is thereby caused to move accidentally.

5. A ball moved by enemy action may be replaced as near as possible to where it lay, or, if lost or destroyed, a ball may be dropped not nearer the hole without penalty.

6. A ball lying in any crater may be lifted and dropped not nearer the hole, preserving the line to the hole, without penalty.

7. A player whose stroke is affected by the simultaneous explosion of a bomb or shell, or by machine-gun fire, may play another ball from the same place, penalty one stroke.

Queer Local Rules

The Duke of Windsor, who has played on an extraordinary variety of the world's courses, once took advantage of a local rule at Jinja in Uganda and lifted his ball from a hippo's footprint without penalty.

Another local rule in Uganda read "If a ball comes to rest in a dangerous proximity to a crocodile, another ball may be dropped."

At the Glen Canyon course in Arizona a local rule provides that "If your ball lands within a club length of a rattlesnake, you are allowed to move the ball." It would be no surprise if players under these circumstances gladly opted for the "unplayable ball" rule.

Signs that have been seen in Africa intimate that "Elephants have right of way" and warn "You are in wild animal country."

71 72 73 74 75 10 9 8 7 6 5 4 3 2 1